■■SCHOLASTIC

Partner Reading

A Way to Help All Readers Grow

Allyson Daley

New York ❖ Toronto ❖ London ❖ Auckland ❖ Sydney **Teaching**
Mexico City ❖ New Delhi ❖ Hong Kong ❖ Buenos Aires *Resources*

Acknowledgments

I would like to give thanks to many of the people who helped me write my first book.

❖ Thank you to principal Liz Phillips and my colleagues at P.S. 321 in Brooklyn, New York, for sharing their ideas and modeling the best literacy practices in their classrooms each and every day.

❖ Thank you to Lucy Calkins and all the amazing staff developers of the Teachers College Reading and Writing Project, Columbia University, for their expertise and research on implementing outstanding reading and writing practices in a primary classroom. Special thanks to Kathy Collins, Kathleen Tolan, and Carl Anderson, the staff developers I was fortunate to work closely with while teaching first grade at P.S. 321.

❖ Special thanks to all my students who eagerly engaged in reading partnerships and allowed me to include their work, voices, and photographs in my book. I am especially grateful to Robert Maass, a professional photographer and parent of one of my students, who expertly took many of the photographs included in the book.

❖ I also want to thank my editor, Sarah Longhi, who encouraged me to write this book and continually offered insightful suggestions to my drafts that helped me shape this book.

❖ Most of all, I am grateful for my family and friends whose constant patience, understanding, and support gave me the motivation and confidence to pursue this journey of writing my first book.

Bibliography and literature search by Rebecca Zerkin
Cover design by Jaime Lucero
Cover photo by Ted Horowitz/CORBIS
Interior design by Kelli Thompson
ISBN: 0-439-51888-1

Table of Contents

Introduction

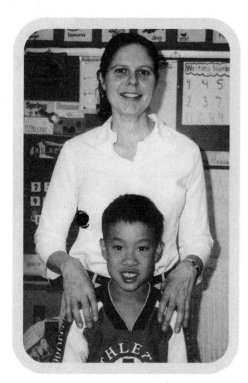

When I began teaching first grade at P.S. 321 in Brooklyn, New York, I was surprised to learn how much time and credibility was given to partner reading—and how successful the literacy program was. Yet I had reservations about partner reading: I thought I had an understanding of reading partnerships and had seen few benefits when I attempted to employ them with my first graders while teaching in a traditional literacy program in Connecticut.

With support and practice, I soon discovered that my initial understanding of reading partnerships was based on a number of misconceptions—and because of these misconceptions, I had implemented partnerships in ways that did little to support my young readers. For instance, I had

◆ paired up students without much consideration for their individual reading abilities. (In fact, I often paired a struggling reader with a fluent reader in hopes that all partnerships would finish reading at the same time.)

◆ required all partnerships to read the same text (an anthology from our mandated basal reading program), even though their reading levels varied greatly.

◆ asked students to respond independently to stories by writing responses to scripted comprehension questions rather than by engaging in book talks with one another.

While teaching at P.S. 321, I had the opportunity to study the authentic practices of reading partnerships within balanced literacy classrooms. The master teachers in these classrooms taught me about the conditions students need in order to become literate, based upon the work of Brian Cambourne (1988). In his research Cambourne identifies the stages students need to go through when becoming literate. According to Cambourne, students need to be immersed in a literary environment, taught specific reading and writing skills that are modified to meet their individual needs, given frequent opportunities to practice what is taught, expected to participate, held accountable for their learning, and provided with ongoing feedback about their performance.

My experiences while teaching at P.S. 321 have taught me that in order to best provide my students with an environment for literary learning as outlined by Cambourne, it is essential to implement a daily literacy model into the classroom. The day-to-day structure of the balanced approach includes time to read and write to students (read alouds, morning message), read and write with students (guided reading, shared reading, and interactive writing), and have students read and write on their own and in small groups (independent reading, partner reading, writing workshop).

My work with partner reading has been one of the most eye-opening changes in my literacy instruction. I am fascinated by the way young readers can not only build basic print skills such as directionality and decoding with the assistance of a partner, but also push a partner to delve deep into a book to find the connections that engage them. Partner reading has become not only a successful, but also an indispensable component of my literacy teaching.

This book is geared toward fellow primary-grade teachers. It both explains the rationale for beginning partnership reading (or reshaping a traditional partner reading practice) and details the important management and instructional strategies for helping students become successful reading partners—and grow individually as readers.

I have organized the chapters to guide you and your students through the implementation and practices of reading partnerships. Chapter 1 defines and outlines how partnerships fit into the daily literacy model. Chapter 2 describes how to organize and prepare students for working in partnerships. Chapters 3 and 4 suggest a series of mini-lessons beginning with teaching students the structure and expectations of partnerships and moving them toward good talk habits and strategies. Chapters 5 and 6 look in depth at a specific type of reading partnership called reading centers. Finally, Chapter 7 examines a variety of methods to use when assessing the work of reading partnerships.

I encourage you to refer to this book as often as needed to find a multitude of strategies, tools, and tips for making reading partnerships a rewarding and indispensable part of your reading program. The power and promise of reading partnerships awaits you!

Balanced Literacy

- ◆ Reading and writing to children
- ◆ Reading and writing with children
- ◆ Reading and writing by children
- ◆ Word study

Chapter 1

Reading Partnerships: An Essential Part of a Balanced Literacy Program

Julia and Jonathon, two first graders, are reading and talking about the book *Minnie and Moo Go to the Moon* by Denys Cazet.

Julia: I don't think the two cows, Minnie and Moo, did the right thing when they didn't tell the farmer the truth about crashing his car into the pigpen.

Jonathon: Maybe they were afraid he would be really angry because they took his jeep without asking and crashed into his pigpen. I think I know how they feel. Sometimes, I'm afraid to tell my parents if I break something. Aren't you?

Julia: Yes, but if it's an accident and you say you're sorry they usually don't get too mad. And anyway, the farmer is going to figure out they did it because he saw Minnie wearing one of his boots and he will find the one which flew off and landed in the pigpen. Look at the picture.

Jonathon: Uh-oh. Let's keep reading and find out if the farmer notices the missing boot . . . .

In my classroom, interactive and reflective conversations about books, like the one captured above, happen on a daily basis among my first graders. My students are self-motivated and eager to talk about books they hear and read all day long.

How do students learn to talk this way about books? What motivates students to pause while reading and reflect about books? Can all students engage in meaningful and purposeful conversations about books?

These are questions I grappled with for many years as a primary teacher until I learned how reading partnerships can be a powerful tool for literacy learning. The pages that follow will demonstrate how reading partnerships provide a motivating format and critical practice for students as they learn to think and talk about books.

What Are Reading Partnerships?

Nika, one of my first graders, defines reading partnerships as follows: "A reading partner is someone you get to spend time with every day. You read and talk about really good books with them. Reading partnerships are fun because you have a friend to talk with about the books you're reading."

Specifically, reading partnerships are pairs of students who read together. Teachers create partnerships by grouping together students with similar reading abilities. (These partnerships, however, are flexible and change throughout the school year as the needs and abilities of students develop.)

As Nika explains, reading partnerships promote a balance between time spent reading and time spent talking about books shared. Students engage in meaningful and purposeful book talk as a result of teacher instruction and frequent practice of these skills. (Chapters 3 and 4 outline mini-lessons to use when teaching students how to develop the skills and habits of "good talk.")

The books partners share are typically on or near the appropriate reading level of the students. My students, for example, use their independent reading books, gathered from our various classroom libraries, for partner reading.

Reading partnerships may occur on a daily basis as one of the fundamental components of your reading block. Other models incorporate partner reading two to three times a week to allow time for students to practice modified partner-based reading practices such as reading centers. (Chapters 5 and 6

define reading centers and suggest a series of mini-lessons for implementing reading centers.) During all partnership experiences, students are paired up and actively engaged in reading and talking about a wide variety of texts.

What Are the Values and Purposes of Partner Reading?

By studying and then implementing reading partnerships into my reading program, I have witnessed marked growth in my students' abilities to discuss and understand books they are reading.

The benefits of partner reading for teachers and students are impressive and include the following:

◆ *Students read more.* By engaging in both independent reading and partner reading, the block of time students spend reading is extended. Having students daily engage with both practices of reading, students increase their stamina as readers. Furthermore, as the year goes on and students mature, partners are able to stay together for longer and longer periods of time each day, mastering the skills of reading and learning and deepening their book talk.

◆ *Students are engaged with a wide variety of books.* Since both partners share their individual book bags (four to five texts at their independent reading level), partners are exposed to twice as many books as they are in independent reading. And as students "shop" for new books each week, there is a continuous flow of new texts for the partners to share. Many of the books chosen by students for their book bags span genres, including fiction, nonfiction, poetry, biography, mysteries, and folk tales.

◆ *Students work cooperatively.* Partners are responsible for deciding together what books to read and how to read them. Through practice, students learn to discuss these choices and make compromises that satisfy both partners.

◆ *Students gain independence and self-confidence through the decision-making opportunities they are given during partner reading.* Some of these decisions include deciding the focus of the talk and making reading plans.

◆ *Students engage in book talk.* Partners learn to listen to each other and engage in conversations that are interactive, rather than parallel. They learn to respond to and build on each other's ideas as well as

introduce new ones. Partners have meaningful book talk with all texts, including simple ones. (In fact, books at the guided reading levels of A, B, and C are great to use with all readers when first practicing book-talk skills. Since these books have limited text, partners are compelled to study and talk about the illustrations to understand the story, since the majority of the story happens in the pictures rather than in the written words.)

◆ *Partners are held accountable by one another for talk that deepens the understanding of a book and the bigger ideas beyond the text.* Students learn ways to encourage partners to extend their thinking and talking.

◆ *Reading partnerships support all readers but are particularly useful for struggling readers.* Struggling readers need additional support, guidance, and practice with print, which partner reading provides on a frequent and consistent basis.

◆ *Partner reading supports the Reading Habits literacy standard of New York City's* Primary Literacy Standards, *which are based on the National Center on Education and the Economy's* New Standards: Performance Standards, *and* Standards for the English Language Arts, *developed by the National Council of Teachers of English and the International Reading Association.* The purpose of the standards is to establish a balanced approach in the teaching of reading and writing in the primary grades. Specifically, the reading habits standard sets the expectation for teachers to read to students (for example, through read alouds), read with students (shared reading, guided reading), and have students read on their own or in small groups (partner reading, independent reading).

How Partner Reading Fits Into a Balanced Literacy Program

In my classroom, I use a workshop approach to teach all the various reading and writing practices previously described. Reading partnerships are one key structure of my reading workshop. Partner reading fits in between guided reading (small groups)/independent reading and literacy centers/individual reading conferences blocks. The advantage of having students either participating in a guided reading group or reading independently first is that they have time to practice reading books and to select those they want to read with their partner.

> ### Values and Purposes of Partner Reading
>
> ◆ Students build reading skills and stamina.
> ◆ Students are engaged with a variety of new books each week.
> ◆ Students work cooperatively and develop communication skills.
> ◆ Students are engaged in book talk that deepens comprehension skills.
> ◆ Students are held accountable for the rigorous work involved with reading and talking.

OUTLINE OF A TYPICAL MORNING LITERACY BLOCK

8:45–9:00 AM Morning Meeting
We read numerous texts including the morning message, calendar, daily schedule, class home-school travel journal, and so on.

9:00–9:15 AM Read Aloud
I alternate between reading chapter books and picture books to my students. I often read texts related to one of our current reading, writing, social studies, or science studies.

9:15–9:25 AM Shared Reading
- We chorally read big books, sing songs, and chant poems printed on charts.
- I use our shared reading time to introduce a reading strategy or skill (e.g., using pictures to help read unknown words, reading with expression, retelling a story using character names, retelling a story across your fingers).
- I use the same shared-reading text over four or five consecutive days. Each day we chorally read the text. This rereading familiarizes students with the words and the meaning and enables them to focus on the skill or strategy that I teach in the shared reading lesson.

9:25–10:35 AM READING WORKSHOP

9:25–9:35 AM Mini-Lesson
In this short instructional period, I explicitly teach a reading strategy for a particular skill. This provides the focus and expectation for what students will practice independently.

9:35–9:50 AM Guided Reading/Independent Reading
- I work with a small group of students on reading a guided reading text. I take anecdotal records of students' oral reading as I sit and listen to each student read.
- Students who are not in the guided reading group are independently reading their bag of leveled texts at their tables.
- All students are practicing the strategy introduced during the day's mini-lesson.

Shared Reading Tip

Think of shared reading as a preview of what will be taught in an upcoming reading workshop mini-lesson. I use shared reading as a time to provide multiple opportunities to demonstrate a strategy to students, providing a great deal of instructional support—it is essential for students to practice new skills and strategies alongside the teacher before they can be expected to practice it independently in the reading workshop.

9:50–10:10 AM Partner Reading/Partner Conferring

📖 My students engage in partner reading, practicing a variety of reading strategies including both those taught during that day's workshop as well as strategies they have learned in previous workshops.

📖 I confer with approximately four partnerships each day, recording observations of each partnership's reading and talking.

10:10–10:30 AM Literacy Centers/Individualized Reading Conferences

📖 I typically confer one-on-one with five students each day. During these conferences, students read several texts from their bag of books. I engage students in conversations about the books to assess their comprehension. I also use this time to provide instruction on strategies that meet students' individual needs and abilities. At the end of the conference we determine which texts each student will exchange from the leveled library. I use my anecdotal records to determine the reading level of the new books the student will choose from the leveled library.

📖 The other students in my class are engaged in pairs, working at literacy centers which include Reading the Room, Writing the Room, Making Words, Solving Poetry Puzzles, Reading Big Books, and playing the games Word Bingo, Word Memory, and Make a Word.

10:30–10:35 AM Reading Share

My class gathers on the carpet for the workshop share. Depending on the focus of the day's mini-lesson, I may choose two students to demonstrate the desired strategy.

10:35–11:35 AM WRITING WORKSHOP

I continue my morning literacy block with the writing workshop, which includes shared reading, interactive writing, the writing mini-lesson, independent writing, individualized writing conferences, and a workshop share.

> **Scheduling Tip**
>
> I have found it most helpful when developing my daily instructional schedule to teach my reading and writing workshops in the morning when my students are most alert and energized.

The literacy block typically spans our morning. In the afternoon, students continue to read and write in other areas of the curriculum, including math, science, and social studies, which I also teach using the workshop model.

The Workshop Format

- Mini-lesson
  (5–10 minutes)
- Student Practice
  (30–45 minutes)
- Share (5 minutes)

The workshop approach can be used to teach all areas of the curriculum.

Reading Workshop in Action

◆◆◆◆◆◆◆◆◆◆◆◆◆◆◆◆◆◆◆◆◆◆◆◆◆◆◆◆◆◆

The following is an example of a typical reading workshop in my first-grade classroom. Notice how the partnership reading focus is determined by the workshop mini-lesson. The mini-lesson, which engages all the students, provides the teaching and practice of the strategy students will be expected to use in their partnership reading. In effective mini-lessons, teachers demonstrate the target strategy with a book that is familiar to students and then provide a few minutes for students to practice with a partner.

◆ THE READING WORKSHOP MINI-LESSON ◆

The class gathers on the carpet in our meeting area. I display the big book *Oh, No!* on an easel for all students to view. (The text is familiar to students since it has been used previously in shared reading.)

Daley: Let's all read the title of this book.

Class: (*chorally*) Oh, No!

Daley: What do you see after the word "No" in the title? (*I point to the exclamation mark.*)

Joshua: An excited mark.

Daley: Why do writers sometimes use excited or exclamation marks?

Caiti: To show how a character is feeling, like maybe mad or sad or really excited.

Daley: Let's take a quick picture walk to refresh our memory of this book that we read together a few days ago. Look closely at the illustrations and try to decide how the character is feeling.

Class takes a picture walk of the text.

Daley: What did you notice during our picture walk?

Students listen and watch as I demonstrate how to read with expression during a mini-lesson.

Brianna: I noticed the girl is upset because she keeps getting holes in everything, like her shirt, skirt, balloon, and bowl. She looks a little mad. She is frowning and scrunching up her face.

Daley: Okay, so we know she is mad because all of her things are getting ruined. Let's try to make our voices sound angry and frustrated like we imagine hers does.

Class chorally practices reading a line of the text using an angry voice.

Daley: Let's have a few volunteers demonstrate how their voice should sound when they read the sentence "Oh, no!" on pages three and four.

Several students volunteer to read a page of the text, altering their voice tone and level when they read the sentence "Oh, no!"

Daley: Now we are ready to read these pages together. Remember, change your reading voice every time the girl says "Oh, no!" so the audience will understand how upset she is.

Class chorally reads the first six pages as I point to the words.

Daley: Today, during your independent and partner reading, I want you to think carefully about what is happening to the characters in your books. Think about how they are feeling and what their voices should sound like. Remember to look for punctuation clues, like the exclamation marks in the book *Oh, No!* Try to match your reading voice to the way the character feels. I will be listening for some amazing reading voices when I confer with partnerships and guided readers today, so go try it!

◆ STUDENT PRACTICE TIME ◆

In the next three instructional blocks of reading workshop, students practice the mini-lesson focus.

Guided reading/Independent reading

While students are independently reading their books with an expressive voice, I work with a guided reading group on a text where punctuation is used to show how the characters are feeling.

Partner reading/Partner conferring

Students engage in partner reading, discussing, and practicing character voices in texts, while I confer with several partnerships. I am specifically observing and providing feedback on their attempts at matching their reading voices to the character's mood.

Literacy centers/Individualized reading conferences

Students engage in literacy centers while I confer one-on-one with several students. The reading conferences focus on the individual needs of the student, including the student's ability to read texts with appropriate character tone and expression.

◆ SHARE ◆

The class gathers on the carpet in the meeting area. I choose two students to demonstrate the skill of reading with an expressive character voice. (I typically choose students who I have conferred with in a partnership, individualized conference, or guided reading group.) Student volunteers read several pages of their text using an expressive voice. Students share the clues they found in the text that helped them determine the character's mood and voice tone.

Alternative Models for Integrating Partnership Reading

◆◆◆◆◆◆◆◆◆◆◆◆◆◆◆◆◆◆◆◆◆◆◆◆◆◆◆◆◆◆◆◆◆◆◆◆◆

I created the workshop model described earlier to best suit the needs of my students. I find it developmentally appropriate, for instance, to have first graders change activities approximately every 20 minutes. I also incorporate literacy practices that allow students to move around the room; having students choose a partner reading space in the classroom and allowing them to work in an alternate body position (cross-legged) is a response to their physical needs.

However, there are many alternatives to this workshop format. You'll want to design a literacy model that works best for your classroom and students. Some things to consider include determining how much time is allotted for each component of your daily reading/writing program and the sequence of activities. The goal in all classroom models is finding a balance between independent and other types of reading, such as partner reading.

Several of my colleagues who teach first grade, for example, prefer to have partner reading precede independent reading each day. They feel it is helpful for struggling readers to have partners work on books together before reading the books independently. Also, some have their students sit side by side for partner reading and then simply turn and sit back to back for independent reading. This technique reduces the transition time from one activity to the other.

Other teachers prefer to have their entire reading block focused solely on independent reading, partner reading, or guided reading. In these classrooms, for instance, partner reading would happen on Mondays and Tuesdays, when the students' book bags hold new books from the leveled library. Independent reading would occur on Wednesdays and Thursdays, when the students are more familiar with their bag of books. Finally, on Fridays, the teacher would meet with all the guided reading groups.

◆

Partnership reading is a tool that, when combined with guided reading, independent reading, shared reading, and read aloud, can reinforce and help students build critical skills in reading and in thinking and talking about texts. Specifically, partner reading provides the peer-learning angle of a literacy program and complements the learning structures you may already have in place. The next chapters describe how to prepare for and successfully manage reading partnerships to maximize your students' learning.

Choosing Your Workshop Format

There are reasons to vary the order of the components of your literacy model. In every model it is most important for students to have time to read alone and time to read with others.

Chapter 2

Getting Your Students and Classroom Ready for Reading Partnerships

Before you make reading partnerships a regular part of your literacy program, you'll want to consider the following: how to pair students, how to create flexible partnerships that meet students' needs, how to select and organize materials that will support partnerships, and how to teach students to select books appropriate to their level and interests. This chapter helps you organize and prepare for partner reading.

How Will I Pair Up My Students?

Daily reading partnerships pair two readers at about the same reading level. Ability-based pairing is especially important in primary grades because these partnerships are meant to support readers as they actually process print. Consequently, the partners need to be able to read the same book jointly or take turns reading. This pairing helps both partners lean toward independence. If, however, one student is a much stronger reader than the other, the stronger reader tends to do most of the work and gets most of the practice. I want students to think of partnerships as opportunities to "work with someone who likes to read the same kinds of books" rather than as responses to their reading levels.

Make sure to use both formal and informal assessments when you create partnerships. Some of the assessment tools I use include the following: ECLAS (New York City's districtwide literacy assessment), running records, and anecdotal data gathered during independent and partner reading conferences as well as during guided reading sessions. (Assessment ideas are included on pages 28 and 29. Chapter 7 provides additional assessment strategies and tips.) The data I gather from these various assessments help me make good decisions about pairing students who have similar reading skills and abilities. I also keep in mind the behavior of students, which is extremely important when asking students to work together in a peaceful and productive way.

Will I Change Partnerships During the Year?

Partnerships, like guided reading groups, should be flexible and can be changed throughout the year. Some teachers change partnerships monthly while others have students in yearlong partnerships.

When deciding whether to change or continue an existing partnership, there are several variables to consider.

First, take into account how the students are working together. (Are they staying on task? Staying focused? Following the guidelines of partner reading?) Two loud, aggressive students put together will most likely *not* result in a calm and productive partnership. Stay flexible; sometimes a partnership is simply not a good match and the students will benefit from changing partners.

Second, note how well the partners know each other as readers and their ability to help each other with partner work. For example, are the partners able to suggest reading strategies that their partner has used successfully in the past when faced with an unknown word? Can the partners engage each other in book talk and help each other keep the talk going? (Chapters 3 and 4 outline mini-lessons to use when teaching students how to develop the skills and habits of "good book talk.")

Third, be aware of each student's reading progress and growth when considering whether to change or maintain an existing partnership. I use my anecdotal records from our guided reading groups and individualized conferences to determine if partners are no longer at or near the same reading ability; then I make changes accordingly.

It is interesting later in the year, after students have had the experience of working with several partners, to give students the chance to choose

their reading partner. This requires some teaching about the etiquette of partnerships, such as how you avoid making a classmate feel rejected, how you say "no" nicely, and so on. (*Source: Principal Elizabeth Phillips, P.S. 321 Staff Handbook*)

What Materials Will My Students and I Need for Partner Reading?

The materials that students need for reading partnerships are simple but essential. They include:

Book Bags: Resealable, gallon-size plastic bags to store independent reading books. I ask class families to donate bags at the start of the year. Some teachers prefer their students to use cardboard magazine file boxes to store their independent books. (I prefer plastic bags because they are less expensive and require less storage space.).

Book Baskets: An assortment of colored plastic baskets to hold and organize sets of books, including those that are leveled by difficulty (guided reading levels A–J) and those that are grouped by topic. (See "Kinds of Book Baskets" on pages 19 and 20.)

You'll need **book leveling guides** to sort your library books accurately by level. I recommend the following resources by guided reading experts Gay Su Pinnell and Irene C. Fountas: *Guided Reading: Good First Teaching for All Children; Matching Books to Readers: Using Leveled Books in Guided Reading, K–3* and *Leveled Books for Readers: Grades 3–6*. These resources list many children's book titles and their corresponding guided reading levels.

Students choose "just right" books from the guided reading leveled baskets. The books chosen are those at the independent reading level of the student.

KINDS OF BOOK BASKETS

When I create book baskets, in addition to my A–J guided reading leveled-book baskets, I consider student interests, reading levels, and class units of study in the areas of writing, math, science, and social studies. Book baskets should be changed throughout the year, for example, when a new study begins. I've found that displaying too many baskets around the room can over-whelm students and slow down the time it takes to choose books, so I recommend replacing baskets rather than continually adding more to your room.

In addition to choosing books from the leveled library baskets, students also pick one or two books from genre, topic, and author baskets to add to their book bag.

The following is a list of suggested book baskets. The read-aloud, mini-texts, and last year's goodies baskets are especially helpful for struggling readers because these books are ones they have had previous experiences with. Struggling readers can easily use these familiar books during partner reading by retelling the stories page by page and engaging in book talk without getting weighted down by the print work. All students enjoy sharing familiar texts because they feel confident using them.

📖 Read-Aloud Book Basket

Every time I finish a read aloud, I add it to the read-aloud basket.

📖 Big Book Mini-Texts

For many of our shared reading experiences I use big books from the Wright Group's Story Box Series. These simple texts have few words and rely heavily on sentence patterns. With each big book comes a set of smaller text copies. Students love using both the big books and the mini-books for partner reading.

KINDS OF BOOK BASKETS (CONT.)

📖 Last Year's Goodies

I always find it helpful to have a few baskets of books that the students worked on the previous year. At my school, for example, all the kindergarten classes participate in author studies of books written by Donald Crews, Eric Carle, and Erza Jack Keats. Also, all the kindergarten classes use the texts recommended by Elizabeth Sulzby (1986) as part of her emergent literacy program (e.g., *Corduroy* by Don Freeman, *Leo the Late Bloomer* by Robert Kraus, and *Brown Bear, Brown Bear* by Bill Martin), so I collect copies of those as well. (In the Sulzby program, students are taught how to read texts by having repeated opportunities to hear and practice retelling the familiar texts. The goal of the program is for each retelling to be a closer approximation of the actual text. Due to the intensive work of the program, students feel extremely confident and comfortable reading these books.)

ABC book baskets

📖 ABC/Alphabet Books

I find these books range from very simple to very complicated and help to meet the wide range of student reading abilities, especially at the start of the school year. (Chapter 6 outlines a full unit of study for partners in reading centers with ABC books.)

📖 Favorite Characters

Books with popular and familiar characters such as Henry and Mudge, Clifford, and Frog and Toad are great books to use in book baskets as well.

📖 Math Book Baskets

I gather books and create baskets related to our math concepts of shape, number, counting, adding, subtracting, time, and measurement.

📖 Science and Social Studies Book Baskets

I gather and create book baskets of fiction and nonfiction books related to our studies. For example, during our insect study I have baskets of books about ants, bees, butterflies, mealworms, ladybugs, and so on. Each time a new study begins I replace existing baskets. This way there is a constant supply of new, exciting books.

How Will My Students Choose Books?

◆◆

Typically, you'll want each student to keep between four and six books in his or her book bag. As mentioned previously, these books are at the student's independent reading level—some are selected from the student's guided reading group materials and others are independent choices.

Books that the student has worked on during recent guided reading lessons make excellent book bag choices. With additional practice and rereading, the guided reading texts—originally at the student's instructional reading level—become independent reading texts.

If you use leveled book baskets, have students choose a few new books at their level each week when they meet with you. I meet with my students at least once a week for an individualized reading conference. (I meet more frequently, however, with struggling readers.) During these conferences, I have students read to me while I provide support and assess their reading skills, needs, and strengths. At the end of each conference, I ask students to separate their books into two piles: those they can read fluently or "smoothly" and are ready to "trade in" to the leveled library and those they want to keep and continue to practice reading. (When a student requires a lot of support with a book, I encourage him or her to keep that book to practice.) Over the course of the year, you'll find that students' frequent use of tools like the Just-Right charts (page 23) helps them become very capable of determining which books they will be able to read easily and identifying those with which they are likely to struggle.

At the end of reading conferences, show students from which leveled basket to choose new books. In this way, students have a new set of books for the week. This system helps me with record keeping and ensures that students make excellent choices: I record all the book titles students choose, and I listen to students read several books before deciding which leveled basket they should read from next. An alternative strategy is to have a designated "shopping day for books" in which, for example, students choose new books every Monday morning.

Have each student also choose one or two books from other types of book baskets around the classroom. At the start of the year, for example, our math book baskets include number books, counting books, pattern books, and so on. (Refer to "Kinds of Book Baskets" on pages 19 and 20 for additional suggestions.) My students are always eager to have the responsibility and freedom of choosing from a selection of baskets.

Book Bag Tips

- Fluent readers may have longer and therefore fewer books in their bag.
- Emergent readers sometimes prefer to keep books they can read easily, and perhaps have even memorized. This is fine, since the rereading of these familiar texts promotes fluency and builds self-confidence. As long as they have some new books to practice with, keeping a few "easy" ones as safety blankets certainly won't do any harm.

◆ ENCOURAGING STUDENTS TO EXPLORE THE CLASSROOM LIBRARIES ◆

The libraries you create for your students and classroom are structured on personal choices. (Some teachers prefer their students to be involved with creating book baskets. They do this by giving small groups of students random piles of books and asking the students to decide how these books could be sorted into libraries.) However you create your classroom libraries, your students need time and repeated opportunities to explore the baskets so they are aware of the books available to them.

Baskets displayed around the room change as new units of study are taught in science, social studies, math, and reading.

Whenever I have a new basket of books, I gather my students together, show them the books in the basket, and then read a few as read alouds. This usually piques their interest and raises their awareness of the kind of books in the basket. We also establish a place in the room where that basket will be kept, so that students can easily locate it when choosing their books.

At the beginning of the school year, I take note of the number of book baskets I have around the classroom. (I put my baskets of leveled texts A–J in one area; five to six math baskets in the math area; five to eight science and social studies baskets in an area; and five to ten baskets such as author, read aloud, and ABC around our reading area and meeting area.) I find it helpful to spend the first weeks of independent reading having small groups of students explore individual baskets of books. During this time, I can assess students individually to determine their reading abilities and they can become familiar with the book baskets around the room.

◆ TEACHING STUDENTS TO CHOOSE "JUST RIGHT" BOOKS ◆

Except for the guided reading leveled libraries, the majority of collections in the book baskets available to your students will be based on a subject matter (e.g., math concept, favorite character) and will consist of collected books with a variety of reading levels. In order for students to choose books that correspond to their reading level, students must be taught to distinguish among books that are "too hard," "too easy," or "just right."

To teach my students how to select books close to their independent reading level, I use the charts shown here, visual aids, and vocabulary to differentiate among the phrases "too hard," "too easy," and "just right."

Typically, I set aside several mini-lessons to role-play how to choose a book by reading several pages of the text. Using the guidelines on the posters, students decide whether the book is too hard, too easy, or just right for me. During one mini-lesson, for instance, I will struggle as I read a text, while during another I will demonstrate reading too quickly, and so on. I also explain to students that when they are deciding whether a text is a "just right" book, they should read the title and the first few pages, rather than the entire book. Following each mini-lesson, provide your students a chance to practice this skill with one of the classroom libraries to ensure their success with selecting appropriate books.

just right
* paying attention to word
* not stuck on every word
* not rushing

too hard
* can't understand words
* reading <u>so, so, so, so</u> slowly

too easy
* reading t<u>oo</u> fast
* not really paying attention

How Will I Teach Students to Have Productive Book Talks?

What exactly is "book talk"? Simply put, "book talk" describes any talk students engage in about the books they are reading.

Book talk is the foundation of reading partnerships. Students need constant experiences talking about books. The daily read alouds you do with your students provide the perfect opportunity for you to model a variety of ways to react and talk about texts. These repeated demonstrations help students build a repertoire of strategies that can carry over into partner reading.

To encourage all students to engage in our read-aloud book talks, I use the phrase "turn and talk to the person next to you" when I want them to think about and discuss things in a story. After only a few days, my students are able to find a nearby "talk partner" quickly, which allows me to stop frequently during our read alouds and start up again easily. My students understand that they are expected to be active participants in our talks. This prepares each student to be accountable for his or her part of the conversation in reading partnerships.

HELPFUL PHRASES TO KEEP BOOK TALK GOING

Teachers can frequently use the questions below during read-aloud book talks so that students can practice thinking and talking about books and become capable of asking these types of questions in their reading partnerships.

Depending on the age and abilities of your students, some questions will be more appropriate to use than others. Here are some questions you may find useful to sustain students' book talks:

◆ What makes you think that?
◆ What makes you say that?
◆ Say more about what you are thinking.
◆ Can you give some evidence for that thinking?
◆ Where are you going with that idea? How does it connect to what we are thinking?
◆ How does that idea/thought help you make sense of what we are reading?
◆ Can you say it again in a different way?
◆ Who can add on to that thought?
◆ Does anyone have a different idea?
◆ Let's try to stay with this idea. Why might that make sense for our discussion?
◆ Can you compare that to what you were thinking earlier?
◆ Okay. You made a connection. How does the connection help you to better understand this book?

(Source: Ginny Lockwood, Teachers College Reading and Writing Project, Columbia University)

Earlier in the year, book talks can be simpler. Some prompts talk partners can respond to include:

◆ Quickly retell what was just read or read the day before.
◆ Describe a picture you have in your mind about a part of the story.
◆ Make a prediction.
◆ Identify a favorite part or character.

As the year progresses, book talks can become more complex. Some additional prompts talk partners can respond to include:

◆ Make connections between books.
◆ Describe how a book connects to your life.
◆ Identify how one part of the book reminds you of another part.
◆ Explain how a book connects to real-world issues.
◆ Share personal responses and reactions to a book.

What Reading Strategies Should I Teach First?

The print strategies you focus on will depend on the grade level and reading abilities of your students. Print strategies are essential because they provide students with ways to attack unknown words. A student's journey toward independence in reading relies on his or her ability to implement a variety of reading strategies when presented with an unknown word. It is common in my classroom during partner reading to hear one student suggest one of the reading strategies outlined below when his or her partner is faced with an unknown word.

As I introduce each print strategy, I record it on a sentence strip and add it to our "Reading Strategies" pocket chart. I display the chart in a highly visible spot so that readers can refer to it often.

In the primary grades, print strategies are explicitly taught and reviewed often. I use our shared reading, read aloud, guided reading, and individualized and partner conferring opportunities to instruct my students on a variety of reading strategies. As a first-grade teacher, I teach reading strategies all year long, but I do have two specific units of study during the months of September/October and January where each reading workshop mini-lesson focuses on strategy work. Descriptions of each print strategy follow.

◆ FIRST UNIT OF STUDY ON PRINT STRATEGIES ◆

1. Look at the book cover.

I demonstrate to students that each time they choose a new book they should look at the cover illustration and attempt to read the title, because often the title words appear in the text. (Read aloud, shared reading, and guided reading are opportunities to demonstrate this practice.)

2. Take a picture walk.

I model for students how to look carefully at each picture in a new text, explaining that pictures help us read words. We practice taking picture walks during read aloud, shared reading, and guided reading. I have found it helpful for my students to verbalize aloud what is happening in each consecutive picture. As students become more adept at taking picture walks, this practice can be done silently.

Picture walks also encourage students to make story predictions, which provide a purpose for their reading (i.e., to find out if their prediction was right).

For struggling readers, the picture walk is the perfect time for teachers to "plant" vocabulary words (i.e., say aloud key words) that are printed on the pages of the text. Consequently, students will be better able to read those words when attempting to read the text in the near future.

As students become fluent readers, you may choose to do very quick picture walks or abbreviated ones where students look only at the first few illustrations.

3. Point to each word as it is read.

When I am teaching students to read, I encourage them to use their "reading finger" to follow the text as they read it. I demonstrate this by using a pointer when we read big books and charts during shared reading.

Tracking the print in texts helps students stay focused, understand book directionality (i.e., top to bottom, left to right), and distinguish among letters, words, and sentences.

Furthermore, this strategy helps teachers highlight for students the reading errors they make (e.g., word substitutions, word omissions, words added in). If, for example, a student reads a sentence and inserts a word, the teacher can reread the sentence, pointing to each word, and illustrate that there is an extra word but nothing to point to. Conversely, if a student omits a word, the teacher can reread the sentence, showing that there is one word left over.

Meeting Students' Needs

Some students will be ready to learn the more complex print strategies earlier than other students. Individualized and partner conferences are excellent opportunities for teachers to introduce new strategies to readers who are ready.

Note that as students become fluent readers, you'll want to move them away from relying on a reading finger, since tracking print with a finger actually slows down the oral reading of a fluent reader. If fluent readers have not naturally stopped using their reading finger, I use the phrase "pull your finger off the page" to remind them.

4. Look at the first letter of the word, make the beginning sound, and think about what makes sense.

When a student is presented with an unknown word, I encourage him or her to make the initial sound of the word, scan the picture for something beginning with that sound and think about words that start with that sound that would make sense in the sentence. The goal is to avoid having students attempt to sound out entire words.

◆ **SECOND UNIT OF STUDY ON PRINT STRATEGIES** ◆

1. Look for chunks in words.

During our word study and spelling lessons, I teach students how to look for smaller words "hiding" inside longer words. We study and practice a variety of spelling patterns (e.g., *at, in, up*). Students understand that seeing *at* in a longer word like *splat* will help them. In fact, they love to be "word detectives" and find smaller words inside of longer ones. (I do explain that sometimes a chunk can be unhelpful, like *he* in *they* or *she*.)

2. Think about what makes sense.

As students become more fluent and the books they read have less picture support, I encourage them to use their comprehension skills and use the context of the surrounding sentence or sentences when faced with an unfamiliar word.

3. Look through words.

When students are presented with longer words, it is important that they think about not only the initial sound but the final and medial sounds as well. If a student, for instance, reads "house" for "home," you can explain that although they start the same, they end differently. This way, you emphasize the importance of the ending and medial sounds of words.

4. Skip and return.

If a student has tried several strategies and none are helping, I encourage him or her to skip the word, read to the end of the sentence, and then go back and try to figure out the unfamiliar word. The context of the sentence often will help students read the unknown word. (Students may need reminders that words they've skipped need to be revisited.)

Print Strategies

- Look at the book cover.
- Take a picture walk.
- Point to words.
- Look at the first letter of words.
- Look for chunks in words.
- Think about what makes sense.
- Look through a word.
- Skip and return.

How Will I Assess Students' Reading Abilities?

As mentioned earlier in the chapter, you'll want to use a variety of formal and informal assessments to determine students' reading abilities. Assessment in my classroom is ongoing and is used to help me pair up students for reading partnerships and to create and modify guided reading groups, as well as to guide my instruction. My students' performance—including their strengths and weaknesses—help me to plan future mini-lessons.

The following is a list of assessment tools I have found beneficial to use with my students:

District or state literacy assessment

ECLAS is a New York City literacy assessment that all teachers are required to administer to their students twice a year until mastery is reached (students achieve specific learning benchmarks). The K–3 literacy strands include phonemic awareness, phonics, reading and oral expression, reading comprehension, reading fluency, listening comprehension, and writing. (Most cities and towns have required literacy assessments for teachers to use that evaluate students on these same literacy strands.) Teachers should also take running records while students read leveled texts (to determine their reading level) and have students respond to books read verbally and in a written format. The goal of any literacy assessment is to discover each student's reading abilities so that the teacher can meet the student's literacy needs through focused instruction.

Running records

During individualized reading conferences, I take running records of students' oral reading and comprehension of texts. Running records allow me to monitor each student's progress and provide assistance on the reading skills and strategies a student may be struggling with. Because we have weekly reading conferences, I always have current data for each student's reading abilities, including his or her strengths, weaknesses, and reading level.

Anecdotal records

Throughout all the components of our daily reading workshop (read aloud, shared reading, guided reading, and individualized and partner conferences), I record observations I make of students' reading strengths and weaknesses. (Chapter 7 contains sample assessment reproducibles I use and keep organized in my reading assessment three-

---

Running Records Resources

You can create your own running record using a book from your leveled library. (Be sure students are unfamiliar with the text so that the assessment will be accurate. In fact, you may want to pull a full set of leveled assessment books out of your classroom library and use them only for assessment.)

Published assessment kits are also available. Two that I recommend are:

◆ *Sunshine Assessment Guide: Grades K–1* (levels A–J) by the Wright Group (www.wrightgroup.com);

◆ *DRA (Developmental Reading Assessment) K–3 Kit* (levels A–M) by Pearson Learning (www.pearsonlearning.com).

ring binder.) These extensive and specific data enable me to keep track of my students' reading abilities and make any needed changes in reading partnerships and guided reading groups.

Self-evaluation

Students, too, can provide valuable information about their reading abilities. At the beginning of the year, during my unit on print strategies, I often ask students to record their names and the strategy they used during that day's workshop. Students place their sticky notes on our class strategy chart (page 25). We discuss our results in our workshop share. This posting process helps students keep track of strategies they have used and it helps me identify students who need additional support. (More self-evaluation strategies and forms for partner reading are provided in Chapter 7.)

When assessing my students, I have learned that to get an accurate profile of a student, the student must be assessed in both formal and informal situations and in a variety of settings (individualized, small group, whole class). Although it can be time-consuming, good assessment is the key to ensuring your students' success as readers because it provides you with the information needed to tailor the curriculum to meet their needs.

◆

Ability-based partnerships can develop students' ability to read and to talk with peers about books. You can help students make the most of partnerships through the background work you do during individual assessments and conferences, read alouds, and mini-lessons: teaching them to choose books that support their reading and interest levels and providing explicit instruction about reading strategies. Reading partnerships stimulate students' reading growth through the daily practice of reading skills (e.g., print strategies, talk practices) that they learn during their reading block. Through a series of mini-lessons, the next chapters outline the step-by-step process of launching partnerships in your classroom, beginning with the fundamental management and structure components and moving toward the teaching of specific talk habits to enhance and support students' reading comprehension.

Chapter 3
Launching Partnerships

Grouping Partners Flexibly

Preparing students for partnerships includes teaching students what to do when their partner is absent or out of the room. A group of three partners may be formed when there is an odd number of students in class, as shown in the photo above.

Once students are familiar with classroom libraries, are capable of choosing books at their independent reading level ("just right" books), have developed a repertoire of reading strategies to use when they come across an unknown word, and have practiced talking about books, they are prepared to begin reading partnerships. (Chapters 1 and 2 outline the strategies students need to learn and practice before working in reading partnerships.) Usually I spend the first three to four weeks of the school year preparing students for partnership work.

In my classroom, I create an atmosphere of great anticipation about partner reading, by excitedly talking about partnerships during the first few weeks of school. I emphasize to students how special partnerships are because everyone gets to work with a classmate reading and talking about wonderful books. (We actually have a day-by-day countdown to the starting of partnerships. This way the first day of reading partners feels like a celebration.)

Teaching Students How to Be Good Partners: Management Strategies and Paired Reading Practices That Support Beginning Partnerships

The following is a list of suggested mini-lessons to teach when you begin partnerships. The first set of mini-lessons focuses on establishing the management and routines of partnerships. The second set focuses on teaching students good book-talk strategies. The sequence of the lessons can be easily rearranged (with the exception of the last one, which is a review). I do, however, recommend that you teach students the management practices of partner reading first so that the guidelines and routines are clear to them. Also, students' prior partnership experiences will determine whether some mini-lessons should be skipped or modified.

◆ BASIC ROUTINES MINI-LESSONS FOR MANAGING PARTNER READING ◆

Mini-Lesson: Where in the room do my partner and I read?

To set the structure for effective partner reading, I teach students to put distance between themselves and other partnerships. I begin the mini-lesson by reviewing how during independent reading, students read their bag of books at their tables. I explain that when students engage in reading partnerships, they choose a place around the room to work. Partners can read together on the carpets or at the tables. By having students physically move to a new reading spot when changing from independent to partner reading, you support their developmental needs as well as signal a transition from one activity to another. During the mini-lesson I have two partnerships role-play sitting too close, in order to help students understand how close proximity between partnerships is distracting.

Mini-Lesson: How do I sit with my partner?

This lesson demonstrates how partners can sit effectively to read together. I use the phrases "side by side" and "knee to knee" to remind students how their bodies should be during partner reading. Sitting side by side and knee to knee allows for a book to be placed on a knee of each partner, which helps keep both partners focused on the book. To demonstrate good partner sitting habits, I use exaggerated role play, as shown in the following mini-lesson excerpt. By exaggerating a reading behavior, I provide students with an engaging visual model that helps them remember which behaviors I expect them to mimic and which they need to avoid.

Ways to Help Students Create Strong Partnerships

- Model positive reading behaviors.
- Name positive reading behaviors.
- Provide time for lots of whole group and partner talks so readers can practice.
- Confer into partnerships.
- Establish rituals for partner reading.
- Foster long-term partnerships.

(Source: Ginny Lockwood, Teachers College Reading and Writing Project, Columbia University)

The class gathers on the carpet in the meeting area.

Daley: Yesterday during our first day of partner reading I noticed the way partners were sitting and I thought today we could practice sitting with partners so we can do our best work. Who would like to volunteer and come up to be my partner?

Mic is chosen to come up to the front of the room.

Daley: Mic, how do you think we should sit so we can share this book?

Mic and the class volunteer different sitting positions, which we try out. Most students suggest sitting cross-legged side by side. Mic and I demonstrate each suggested position while reading a page of text. The class discusses the most effective sitting positions. After this discussion, I demonstrate ineffective sitting positions as I continue with the role play.

Daley: I have another idea. I will sit behind you so we are sitting back to back.

As I demonstrate this ineffective way of sharing a book, the class breaks out in laughter.

Daley: Why are you laughing? I'm sitting next to him like you said.

Joe: Because you can't see the book, so how can you read it?

Daley: Oh, I get it. So maybe we should sit next to each other. Let's try it that way, okay?

This time I sit next to Mic but purposely leave a large gap between the two of us. When we attempt to read the book, I dramatically lean over so I can see the print and then shout the words on the page so Mic can hear me read. The class breaks out into laughter.

Daley: Now why are you laughing? I'm doing what you told me—I'm sitting next to him.

Chelsea: You have to sit so your knees are touching.

Daley: Oh, now I think I really get it. Let's try it once more, Mic.

Mic and I sit side by side, knee to knee, and balance the book between us. We read several pages of the text successfully.

Daley: *(send-off)* Today, I want you and your partner to practice sitting side by side and knee to knee when you are reading and talking.

Mini-Lesson: How do we choose the book(s) to read?

In my classroom, partners bring their individual book bags to their chosen reading spot, where they combine their collections of books. Partners must learn to make decisions cooperatively about which books to share and how to share them so that each gets a turn with a book he or she has chosen. This lesson emphasizes that partners can both talk during book conversations by taking turns.

The class gathers on the carpet.

Daley: Yesterday, I noticed Anna and Nika doing something really great when they were deciding what book to read. I've asked them to show us today what they did.

Nika and Anna come and sit in front of the class with their book bags.

Nika: We decided that it was fair if we took turns choosing a book from our bag each time we read a new book.

Anna: And we decided that each day the other partner would pick first. So today I get to choose the first book because Nika chose the first one yesterday. (*Anna looks in her book bag.*) So today Nika we can start by reading my book, *Poppleton*.

Daley: (*send-off*) Today, I want all of you to try taking turns when choosing books to share with your partner.

Mini-Lesson: What is the book "owner's" responsibility?

Once a partner chooses a book, the two readers look over the book together. Because the book belongs to one of the partners, and the "owner" has most likely already read the book during independent or guided reading, the book's owner does a book introduction for his or her partner. This lesson reminds students of ways to give a good book introduction and establishes the book owner's responsibility to do so. (My students are familiar with book introductions because we practice them with new texts during read aloud, shared reading, and guided reading.)

The class gathers on the carpet.

Daley: I was noticing that yesterday a lot of you were doing something great partners do. You were introducing your book to your partner just like I do whenever we are about to share a new book. What kinds of things could you tell your partner when you are introducing them to one of your books?

I record their suggestions on a chart titled "What Can You Say in a Book Introduction?"

Matthew: The title.

Julia: The author.

Joe: You can talk about the cover illustration.

Caiti: You can take a picture walk.

Sean: You can tell them what the problem will be in the story, but not the solution, so they will want to read and find out what happens.

I choose a pair of students to model a book introduction. Megan and Dan come and sit in front of the class.

Megan: I am choosing the book *Shopping. (She points to the title.)* It's by Joy Cowley. She writes a lot of the books we read.

Dan: Shopping. *(He echo reads the title using his reading finger.)*

Megan: It's a book about a boy and his mom. One day they go grocery shopping. Look at the cover. How can you tell they are going shopping?

Dan: Well, it looks like they are in front of a store window that has bins of food. And the mom is holding a purse with money hanging out of it and you need money when you go shopping.

Megan: Let's take a picture walk and see what they buy at the store.

Megan and Dan go page by page and name the items being put in the grocery cart—eggs, apples, ice cream, toothpaste. They are focused on the illustrations during this time rather than the print.

Megan: I don't want to show you the last page, because it's a surprise about what happens with the boy and the shopping cart. We'll read and then you can find out, okay?

Daley: *(send-off)* Today I want you to try to give your partner a book intro-duction when you are reading one of your books. Think about the great things Megan did with her partner. She talked about the title, the cover illustration, the pictures in the story, the characters, and the setting, and she got Dan curious about the ending without giving it away, so now he is excited to read the book. Wow, they did a great job!

Mini-Lesson: Are you paying attention to your partner?

To convey how important it is to listen to your partner while partners read and talk about a book, I teach several mini-lessons in which I ask a volunteer to be my reading partner. While my partner is reading, I will purposely misbehave. Some misbehaviors you can demonstrate include humming, talking to another partnership, looking at a different book, and so on. My students find these demonstrations hilarious as well as informative. We always spend time discussing why my behavior is problematic and disruptive to the partnership.

◆ PAIRED READING PRACTICES MINI-LESSONS ◆

Mini-Lesson: What are the different ways you can read a book?

After previewing a new book, partners decide how they want to read the text. I have found that granting students the opportunity to make this decision empowers them. They feel a sense of pride in making decisions and therefore take this responsibility seriously. I teach three ways partners can read books:

Choral Reading: Partners read aloud in unison.

> *Taking Turns:* Partners alternate reading chunks of pages. (I prefer to have students read several pages or several sentences, rather than single pages, to help the reader get the rhythm of the text and build fluency.)

> *Echo Reading:* One partner reads a chunk of pages and the other reader rereads the same pages. (I have found echo reading especially beneficial to partnerships with one slightly stronger reader.)

I typically teach a mini-lesson for each way of reading. I demonstrate with student volunteers. I also use the share time to have partnerships demonstrate how they chose to read a book by reading a few pages using the format chosen. I encourage students to alternate these reading methods each day.

Mini-Lesson: How can you help your partner when he or she gets stuck on a word?

When one partner has difficulty reading a word, the other partner can offer help and support without giving away the unfamiliar word. I make a point of insisting that my students not jump in too quickly to help their partner get past a difficult word. My students understand that by giving their partner the word, they are taking his or her turn.

Ways for Partners To Read Books

◆ Chorally
◆ Taking Turns
◆ Echoing

More important, however, I explain that giving a partner the answer won't help him or her for the next time he or she is reading and presented with that same word. I convey to students that they need to wait for their partner "to have a go" at an unfamiliar word. Students can offer suggestions to a struggling partner by suggesting a specific reading strategy, such as looking for a word chunk or looking at the picture.

When Your Partner Gets Stuck On A Word, You Can Say...

- Tell them, "look at the 1st letter."
- Tell them, "Find a little word inside the troubling word."
- Tell them, "Try skipping the word and coming back to it at the end of the sentence."
- Tell them, "Look at the picture."
- Tell them, "Look at the last letter, look at the middle letter." (Looking through a word.)

Sometimes, of course, the student who knows the troublesome word will simply read it for the other partner. Because my readers have many opportunities to process texts on their own (independent and guided reading), I don't worry a great deal over the occasional times when students produce correct words for each other.

Over the course of the year, I have found it helpful to record ways students have helped one another read difficult words. I use partner conferring opportunities to capture prompts that partners use when encouraging one another to figure out difficult words. Periodically, I teach mini-lessons that focus on the kinds of things good readers say to a partner who is faced with a troubling word. I record these "helpful hints" on a chart for students to use.

The class gathers on the carpet.

Daley: Yesterday, I noticed Dana and Siobhan doing something great when one of them got stuck on a word. I asked them to share with us some of the ways they were helping each other

Dana and Siobhan sit in front of the class.

Siobhan: We were reading the book *Animals at the Zoo*. When we got to this page, Dana had trouble with the word *lion*. She was trying to sound it out. I know this word is a rule breaker so I told her, "Look at the picture," and then she got it because she saw the lion in the picture.

Dana: Later, when Siobhan was reading this page, she had trouble with the word *short*. I reminded her of the special sound that *sh* says, like in *shoe* and *shirt* and then she got it.

Daley: *(send-off)* I really think Dana and Siobhan were being smart partners. They were giving each other a helpful reading strategy to use instead of reading the word for each other. Today I want you to give your partner a clue if he or she is stuck on a word. Remember you can use some of the ideas we have listed on our chart to help one another.

Mini-Lesson: Reviewing what a good partner does

After beginning partnerships, it is helpful for students to review the ways they can work best with their partner.

The class gathers on the carpet.

Daley: You guys have been doing such amazing work in your partnerships over the past few weeks. I wanted us to take the time today to brainstorm all of the things we do to make our partnerships great, and write them on a chart.

On chart paper, I print the title "What Does a Good Partner Do?"

Who has an idea?

Max: A good partner sits cross-legged, knee to knee.

Caiti: The book should be on each partner's knee so they both can see the words and pictures.

Chelsea: Partners take turns choosing books to read.

Matthew: Partners talk about how they want to read a book like maybe together [chorally], or by taking turns, or by echoing each other.

Mic: Partners listen to each other when they read.

Julia: Partners treat books nicely.

Andy: Partners find quiet places to read away from other partnerships.

Daley: *(send-off)* Today, I want you and your partner to make sure you are trying four or more good partnership behaviors. If you forget some, look on our chart. We'll share which ones you tried during our workshop share.

What Does a Good Partner Do?

- Finds a quiet reading spot.
- Sits side by side, knee to knee.
- Balances the book on each partner's knee.
- Takes turns choosing books.
- Reads by echoing, taking turns, or reading chorally.
- Previews a book before reading it.
- Listens when a partner reads.
- Looks at a partner when he or she is talking about a book.
- Treats books with respect.
- Gives wait time and clues when a partner is stuck on a difficult word.

Teaching Beginning Partnerships Good Talk Habits

Once your students have an understanding of the routines, expectations, and guidelines of partner reading, you are ready to focus on the talk aspect of partner reading for your mini-lessons.

At this point, students are familiar with good talk habits through their experiences talking about books during your frequent read alouds, shared reading, and guided reading experiences, as outlined in Chapters 1 and 2. Partnerships provide students with countless opportunities to engage in frequent and intensive book talks. You can use partner conferring times to assess and support partner talk.

The following is an outline of suggested talk strategies that help you teach students how to talk about books in purposeful and meaningful ways. (As with the mini-lessons presented earlier in the chapter, individual teachers can decide which ones best suit the needs of their students.) Each strategy is illustrated by excerpts from partner talks I've observed.

◆ GOOD TALK STRATEGY # 1: LOOKING CLOSELY AT THE PICTURES ◆

To encourage students to look closely at the illustrations, we spend a great deal of time taking picture walks during our shared reading, read aloud, and guided reading experiences. My goal is for students to practice the strategy frequently.

The Strategy in Action
Partner Conversation #1:
Partners are using the pictures to talk and add to the story.

> **Julia:** You know what I am noticing about this book? Everything is made out of an animal or wood. *(Points and names objects in the picture of the Indian village scene.)* Like their tepee, kayak, and jewelry.

> **Jonathon:** Oh, yeah. And look, their tools and weapons are, too.

> **Julia:** That's unusual because nowadays we use metal mostly.

After reading several more pages.

> **Julia:** And do you see the things that they are painting, like their skin and tepees? Did you know what they used for paint back then?

Jonathon: No.

Julia: They used berries and smushed them. Isn't that cool?

Partner Conversation #2:
Partners are taking a picture walk and comparing the pictures.

Joshua: Do you know what? I think the witches in the story are serious witches because they always have a bat with them and bats are scary and witches sometimes want to be scary.

Brianna: But I think they all start to get nicer as their wishes come true. It looks like in this picture the witches and bats have a half smile on their face, but then on the next pages they all have big smiles.

Joshua: Oh, yeah. Well, let's read and find out if they turn out to be mean or nice witches.

After I have had the chance to confer and record several of these types of conversations that demonstrate good picture talks, I print them either on an overhead or chart paper and share them with my class as mini-lessons. The class reads aloud each conversation and then identifies specific examples from each conversation that show good partnership picture talk.

I keep an ongoing chart to record what they notice.

Ways We Can Talk About Pictures ————————————

- ❖ Notice something interesting in a picture.
- ❖ Notice how the picture helps you read the words.
- ❖ Notice how the picture doesn't exactly match the words.
- ❖ Notice there is more to the story than the words tell you.
- ❖ Notice how the details change in the pictures.
- ❖ Notice how books with good illustrations let you "read" and have a talk based on the pictures only, especially nonfiction books.

◆ GOOD TALK STRATEGY #2: LOOKING CLOSELY AT THE PRINT ◆

To help my students look closely at the words on the page, I use many big books during our shared reading experiences. (The Wright Group's Story Box series is great to use. These big books have limited text on each page and rely heavily on sentence patterns.) My goal is for students to transfer this skill to their work in reading partnerships.

The following are excerpts of partnership conversations I captured, that show students demonstrating good book talk about the print in their texts.

The Strategy in Action
Partner Conversation #1:
Partners focus on similar letters and sounds of character names.

> **Caiti:** I noticed something about the three character names in this book— Wilma, Wanda, and Wendy. They all start with the letter "W."

> **Chelsea:** Yeah, just like our names both start with the same letter, "C." But the "C" in our names makes different sounds. The "W" in their names always sounds the same.

Partner Conversation #2:
Partners notice boldface words in the text.

> **Sean:** I noticed that the author is sometimes writing the words with really dark black.

> **Mic:** Yeah, that means we have to say those words extra loud. Let's reread the book and try that so it sounds the way the author wants. It will show that the man is really mad so he is yelling.

After I have the chance to confer and record several of these conversations that demonstrate good print talk, I print them on either an overhead or chart paper and share them with my class as mini-lessons. The class reads aloud each conversation and then identifies specific examples from each conversation that show good partnership print work.

I keep an ongoing chart to record what they notice.

Ways We Can Talk About Print

- ❖ Notice a sentence pattern in a book and think how it helps you read.
- ❖ Notice when one word keeps repeating. Keep looking for that word.
- ❖ Notice how the print size, color, or shape changes.
- ❖ Notice how punctuation (. ! ? " ") helps you change your voice when you are reading.
- ❖ Notice a favorite word or line in a story or poem.

Fluency Tip

When students struggle to read fluently, have them practice reading simpler texts. This way, they can focus on reading smoothly, rather than struggling with word work. Once they achieve fluency with an easier text, they might return to the original text or continue to build fluency with other books on the level of the easier text.

♦ Good Talk Strategy #3: How Rereading Books Helps You ♦

My students continually reread familiar texts. They understand that by rereading, they become fluent and develop a stronger understanding of the story. From the start of the school year, I encourage students to do repeated readings of books. I model this behavior by using shared texts (big books, charted poems, and songs) over and over while teaching a variety of strategies for reading.

The Strategy in Action
Partner Conversation #1:
A student who has read a book encourages her partner to use prereading strategies.

Siobhan: I can't make a prediction of what is going to happen in this book because I have already read it. Why don't you make one by looking at the cover.

Megan: Okay, and you can tell me if I am on the right track or not.

Partner Conversation #2:
Partners notice how pictures add to the story and the reader's understanding.

Jackson: When I reread this book a second time, I noticed a lot more.

Joe: Like what?

Jackson: Well, the first time I read it, I only looked at the words. I forgot to look at the pictures. When I finished, I was confused about the story so I reread it and remembered to look at the pictures, too. I noticed a lot of things in the pictures that helped me understand what was going on in the story. So today when we read it, let's make sure we spend time looking at the pictures and the words.

After I have the chance to confer and record several of these conversations that demonstrate the benefits of rereading texts, I print them on either an overhead or chart paper and share them with my class as mini-lessons. The class reads aloud each conversation and then identifies how one partner's having already read a text can help the other partner.

Benefits of Rereading Texts

- Rereading supports growth of oral language skills.
- Rereading supports growth of a sense of story.
- Rereading offers a highly supported exposure to a wide variety of books and genres.
- Rereading allows all levels of readers to experience success and engagement.

(Source: Kathy Collins, Teachers College Reading and Writing Project, Columbia University)

I keep an ongoing chart to record what they notice.

How Rereading Books Helps Us to Be Great Readers

❖ We become fluent, smooth readers.
❖ We recognize words quickly.
❖ We understand how the character feels and we can change our reading voices to match those feelings.
❖ We see things in the pictures we didn't notice before.
❖ We understand the story better.
❖ We can retell the story with lots of details.

◆ GOOD TALK STRATEGY #4: THINKING BEYOND THE PAGE ◆

I use read alouds, guided reading sessions, and individualized and partner reading conferences to guide and encourage students to extend their thinking about books beyond the literal level. During these experiences, I model for students that thinking about a book should occur before, during, and after reading a text. Students understand that their thinking about a book will and should change as they read and the story unfolds. I tell them "good readers revise their thinking about books as they read more."

The Strategy in Action
Partner Conversation #1:
Partners make inferences about the text while reading and talking.

Nicholas: *(After reading an entire text.)* I think it was really mean of the dog to jump in the dirt after the kids washed him in the tub.

Siobhan: Yeah, I think he was naughty because he rolled in the dirt two times after they gave him two baths.

Nicholas: If I played in the mud after my bath, my mom would be really mad.

Siobhan: Yeah, I would get in big trouble. But it's okay when you are playing in the sand at the beach and you roll around in the sand, because you can just wash off in the water.

Partner Conversation #2:
Partners develop a big idea about the text being read.

Julia: I think it was really funny in the middle of the book when all the pigs went flying out of the mud because the cows driving the tractor crashed into them. I think that's where the author got his idea for the title, *Pigsty*, because when the crash happened there was a huge mess.

Jonathon: But why did the cows want to drive the tractor in the first place?

Julia: I think maybe they were just having a boring day. I mean, look at the pictures at the start of the book. They have nothing to do except eat the grass. What if all we did all day was eat? We would get bored, too, and maybe end up getting into trouble like the cows.

Jonathon: Yeah. Sometimes when I'm bored at home I start to tease my little brother and then I always get in trouble because he tells. Or maybe the cows are mad at the farmer and want to wreck his stuff on purpose.

Julia: Maybe. The author never really tells us, so I guess he wants us to decide.

Partner Conversation #3:
Partners make connections between books they have read.

Nika: The book we just read, *Leo the Late Bloomer*, reminds me of the book we heard yesterday for read aloud, *The Little Engine That Could*.

Anna: Yeah, because in both books the main character is having a hard time doing stuff that he wants to do.

Nika: Yeah, and then at the end of both books that character can do all the things he was having trouble doing. Like the Little Engine made it over the hill and Leo learned to read and write.

After I have the chance to confer and record several of these conversations that demonstrate partners thinking deeper about books, I print them on either an overhead or chart paper and share them with my class as mini-lessons. The class reads aloud each conversation and identifies examples of how partners are really thinking and talking about books. •

I keep an ongoing chart to record what they notice.

Phrases That Help Us Think Harder About Books ─────────

- ❖ I wonder why . . . .
- ❖ It reminds me of . . . .
- ❖ My favorite character/part is _____ because . . . .
- ❖ I noticed a connection between this book and another we read . . . .
- ❖ I noticed how this book is similar to/different from other books we read . . . .

"HOW CAN WE HAVE GREAT BOOK CONVERSATIONS?"

- ◆ Really notice the pictures.
- ◆ Ask, "What makes you say that?"
- ◆ Notice the words.
- ◆ Read first.
- ◆ Keep the conversation about the book.
- ◆ Listen and pay attention. Look at the person talking.
- ◆ Stop reading when the book doesn't make sense.
- ◆ Ask good questions. Try to answer them.
- ◆ Stick to one topic.
- ◆ Compare books.
- ◆ Compare parts of the same book.
- ◆ Talk before you start to read. You already have ideas.
- ◆ Take a picture walk.
- ◆ Agree, disagree, add on.
- ◆ Don't just say it; prove it with the pictures and words.

(Source: Ginny Lockwood, Teachers College Reading and Writing Project, Columbia University)

Launching reading partnerships is an exciting event for students. Successful partnerships occur through the teaching of simple, well-timed mini-lessons that focus on one strategy at a time to reinforce good reading habits and teach students how to be supportive, effective partners. The routines, management strategies, and good book-talk habits that students learn provide them with a solid foundation for partner work. This work can be revisited later and is expanded upon in the next chapter.

Chapter 4

Extending the Talk:
More Partner Reading Strategies

By midyear, I am ready to teach a second unit of study on partnership work. The purpose of the study is to teach reading partners strategies that will help to extend and focus their book talk and, in effect, increase the time and effort they invest in reading and comprehending. Factors such as the grade level you teach, the partnership experience of your students, and their reading abilities will help you determine whether the mini-lessons suggested in this chapter will need to be modified or taught earlier or later in the school year.

I divide the study of extending partnership talk into two parts: in-the-moment talk and planned talk. In-the-moment talk refers to the talk that spontaneously happens between partners reading a book together. Once partners have had ample opportunities to practice in-the-moment talk, they can engage in planned talk, whereby they set goals for what they'll discuss and how they'll talk before they meet. Learning both types of talk helps students develop strategies that keep their conversations both rich and purposeful.

Teaching Partners How to Extend Their Book Conversations With In-the-Moment Talk

◆◆◆

Begin this study by briefly reviewing with students the book-talk strategies they have already learned to use in their reading partnerships. You might use the class charts "What Does a Good Partner Do?" and "How Can We Have Great Book Conversations?" from Chapter 3 to review your talk strategies. Then explain to students that they are ready to learn more challenging talk practices, which will make their book conversations even more interesting and exciting.

The first step is to help partners make a conversation of their book talk. I tell students that for partners to have great book talks, they need to make sure they are engaged in conversations rather than "shares." (A share is when two partners say things that are unrelated and unconnected to each other's ideas.) Partners engage in conversations when they listen and respond to one another. I use the reading process as an analogy: When students read a book, they listen, think, and then react to the author's words—they have a conversation with the book. Likewise, when partners talk, they must listen, think about what their partner said, and then respond.

You'll want to spend several mini-lessons teaching students ways they can engage in a book conversation (i.e., respond to what their partner says). Some of the strategies presented in the mini-lessons that follow include questioning, disagreeing, asking for clarification, and requesting more information.

◆ MINI-LESSON: EXTENDING BOOK TALK THROUGH QUESTIONING ◆

Below is an example of a conversation I role-played to demonstrate how asking questions can be used to extend book conversations.

Class gathers on the carpet.

Daley: Today, we are going to practice having longer conversations about the books we are reading with our partners. A great way to do this is to ask your partner questions about his or her ideas and comments. I want you to listen to the conversation I am going to have today and see how I keep the conversation going. Listen carefully for the questions I ask my partner. Okay, who wants to be my partner and talk about the book *Lilly's Purple Plastic Purse* by Kevin Henkes, which we read aloud earlier today?

Emily volunteers to be my partner.

Daley: When Emily and I talk about the book, I want all of you to listen carefully and see how I get Emily to stretch out her thinking and talking about the book.

Okay, Emily, let's chat about the book for a few minutes. Why don't you start by telling me something that surprised you when you heard the story.

Emily: Well, I was surprised that Emily wrote such a mean note to her teacher, Mr. Slinger.

Daley: Me, too. Show me that part.

Emily finds the page and reads aloud the letter.

Daley: What surprised you the most?

Emily: That it was so mean and it was for her teacher! I would never write or draw a mean picture like she did about my teacher, even if I was really mad. I wouldn't want to get in trouble! And anyway, it was kind of her fault.

Daley: What do you mean by that?

Emily: It's like our classroom rules. When you bring in something to share, you have to keep it away until it's share time. Mr. Slinger is like you. He takes away her share because she was playing with it when it wasn't share time. Lilly knew the rules but she ignored them. That's why he got mad and took the purse away.

Daley: So do you think *maybe* Lilly should have just waited until share time to take it out and then this wouldn't have happened?

Emily: Yeah, but sometimes it's hard to wait and I think she was worried that they were running out of time. I don't think they have share time at the start of the day like we do.

Daley: Why do you think that?

Emily: (*Looks back and points to the text illustrations.*) Well they were doing so many things like reading and spelling and math that Lilly probably thought the day was going to end before she got a chance to share.

The conversation continues for several minutes, with me encouraging Emily to say more by asking her questions.

At the end of the conversation, I ask the class if they noticed any questions I used to help Emily say more. I record on a chart the questions that the students notice I repeatedly use to encourage my partner to say more. After several mini-lessons, students are able to identify the questions I repeatedly use when having the book conversations.

Strategy #1: Stretch Out Ideas by Asking:

- ❖ "Why do you think that?"
- ❖ "Why do you say that?"
- ❖ "Can you say more about that?"
- ❖ "What do you mean by that?"
- ❖ "Can you show me that part?"
- ❖ "So are you saying . . . ?"

◆ MINI-LESSON: EXTENDING BOOK TALK THROUGH DEBATING ◆

Another helpful talk strategy students can be taught is how to debate ideas with their partner. Students often need to understand that it is acceptable to disagree with a partner's ideas. (I remind students that when they debate or disagree with someone, they need to be respectful and nonjudgmental).

To teach students how to engage in a conversation when partners have different opinions, I choose read alouds that will encourage students to form an opinion when talking about the book. One great book I use is *The True Story of the 3 Little Pigs!* by Jon Scieszka, which is told from the perspective of the Wolf, who claims he has been misunderstood and falsely accused of crimes, and is actually an innocent victim.

Daley: Sometimes when you and your partner read books, you may not always have the same ideas and opinions about the stories. It is okay for partners to disagree about how they feel about characters and the choices they make in a story. Everyone has the right to his or her own feelings, and as partners, you need to listen to one another and respect one another's ideas. Today we are going to practice how we can have great book talks even when we don't agree with our partner's ideas. Who would like to volunteer to talk with me about our read aloud *The True Story of the 3 Little Pigs*?

Joe volunteers to be my partner.

Asking Questions About Texts

Be sure during read aloud and shared reading to model how to ask open-ended questions about books rather than literal-level comprehension questions. Open-ended questions encourage students to share different ideas and opinions. As students react, respond, and add to one another's ideas, an interactive class discussion evolves in which the teacher takes on the role of coach rather than leader.

Daley: Well, Joe, what are you thinking about this story?

Joe: Well, I think the Wolf is lying. He wants everyone to feel sorry for him so he won't be sent to jail.

Daley: Can you say more about that?

Joe: The Wolf knows everyone blames him because they know wolves like to eat pigs so he is trying to trick them into thinking it was an accident. He wants them to feel sorry for him because he was sick.

Daley: Hmmm. I hear what you are saying but I *disagree* with you because I think it's possible that he really had a bad cold and an attack of the sneezes. If the pigs had just taken the time to listen to him when he came to their house, they would have known he just wanted to borrow some sugar.

Joe: But if he was a good wolf, I don't think the pigs would have been so mean to him right away. They would have let him in and given him the sugar he needed.

Daley: Why do you think that?

Joe: Well, if he had been nice to them on other days, then when he came on this day, they would have taken the time to listen to him. He must have been mean to them before so they didn't think they could trust him.

Daley: But they didn't even give him a chance to explain why he had come to their house. They were rude and ignored his knocking. *Maybe* they're the selfish ones and don't like to help others.

Joe: I disagree. They knew the wolf wanted to eat them, so they didn't open their doors, which was a smart thing to do. And they were right because after the first two pigs died when their houses fell down, he ate them! So he should definitely go to jail for that!

Daley: Can you show me that part?

Joe turns to the illustrations in the text.

Daley: Okay, I agree with you that he does like to eat pigs, but I still disagree that he is the only one to blame. If the pigs had been friendlier neighbors and had just listened to him, maybe he could have gotten the sugar and left them alone before anything awful happened.

The conversation continues for several minutes as Joe and I debate whether the Wolf was innocent, using the words and illustrations as evidence to support our thinking.

At the end of the conversation, I ask the class if they noticed any words I used to share my opinions and to get Joe to say more about his opinions. I add to the class strategy chart the phrases that the students notice I use to encourage my partner to engage in a debate. After several mini-lessons, students are able to identify phrases I repeatedly use when I am debating ideas with a partner.

Strategy #2: Debate Ideas by Saying:

- ❖ "I agree . . . I disagree . . . because . . ."
- ❖ "Maybe it's . . . or maybe it's . . ."
- ❖ "It could be . . . or it could be . . ."

◆ MINI-LESSON: EXTENDING BOOK TALK BY MAKING TEXT-TO-SELF CONNECTIONS ◆

Over the course of several mini-lessons, I teach students the different kinds of connections they can make when talking about books as a way to extend their book conversations. I begin with text-to-self connections because these are the easiest connections for students to make. Text-to-self connections are when students relate a character's experience to one of their own.

Since many students naturally make text-to-self connections, I can use conversations I hear when conferring with partners to share with the class in mini-lessons. (I record conversations on chart paper or overheads.)

Daley: I wanted to share with you a conversation I heard between Caiti and Matthew about the book they were reading, *Alexander and the Terrible, Horrible, No Good, Very Bad Day* by Judith Viorst. When I was listening to their talk, I noticed something really interesting that they were doing. Let's read the part of their conversation I wrote on the chart and try to figure out what great thinking and talking they did after they read the book.

Class chorally reads aloud the recorded conversation below.

Caiti: In this part of the story (*she turns to the illustration*), I know how Alexander feels in the book because sometimes my brother is mean to me and starts fighting with me. And then when I yell at him or hit him back, my mom gets mad at me and I'm the one who gets punished.

It's not fair because my brother starts it and then doesn't even get into any trouble. It's the same for Alexander. On this page it shows his brothers making him fall in the mud and calling him a crybaby. And when he punches them back, his mom yells and blames him for fighting and getting all muddy.

Matthew: I know. My brothers always bug me too. Like in this part (*he turns to the illustration*), when Nick and Anthony won't let him have the toy from the cereal box, my brothers do the same thing to me. They always say they are the bosses because they are older. It stinks being the youngest because everyone else gets to tell you what to do all the time.

Daley: What did you notice about the talk Matthew and Caiti were having about their book?

Max: They noticed that the same things happen to them as Alexander.

Siobhan: Yeah. They all have big brothers who pick on them and boss them around just like Alexander.

Daley: Yes, that's right. Caiti and Matthew were thinking about the big things that were happening to the main character and how those things reminded them of their own lives. We call those "connections." Connections help make our conversations interesting and push us to do great thinking. It's really important when you are making connections to use the words and the pictures of your books to guide your talk just like Max and Siobhan did. I am going to add "making connections" to our book-talk strategy chart. Today when you read with your partner, I want you to notice if characters or things that happen in the story are like your life. Go try it.

Over the next few days, I have partners share with the class connections they made with their texts during the share part of the workshop.

Strategy #3: Make Text-to-Self Connections by Asking:

❖ "Does any character remind me of myself? In what way?"
❖ "Did anything happen to one of the characters that reminds me of something that happened in my life?

> ### Teaching Text-to-Self Connections
>
> When teaching students to make self-to-text connections, encourage them to use the words and illustrations in the text they are reading to support their talk. In this way, the talk stays grounded in the text.

◆ MINI-LESSON: EXTENDING BOOK TALK BY MAKING TEXT-TO-TEXT CONNECTIONS ◆

Another type of connection I teach my students to make during book talks is text-to-text connections. Text-to-text connections occur when students compare books and identify ways the texts are similar. Because reading partners read many books together, this strategy can be used frequently.

To teach this strategy, I role-play partner conversations using texts I have recently read aloud.

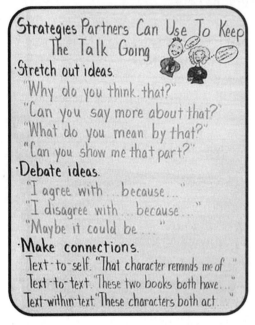

Talk strategies listed on a chart serve as a helpful resource during partner reading time.

Daley: We have been working on making great connections between our lives and the books we have been reading over the past few days. I think we are ready to learn about another kind of connection we can make with the books we are reading. Who would like to help me practice another kind of connection by talking about our read alouds, *There's Something in My Attic* by Mercer Mayer and *Amelia Bedelia* by Peggy Parish?

Brianna volunteers to be my partner.

Daley: I was thinking about these two books after we read them and I was wondering if we could make any connections between them. Can you think of any ways these books are the same? Do any of the characters remind you of another character?

Brianna: Yeah, they do. Both Amelia Bedelia and the little girl do things that surprise the other characters.

Daley: What do you mean by that.

Brianna: Well, in the book *There's Something in My Attic*, the nightmare in this picture looks really surprised and confused when the girl starts yelling at him and trying to capture him with the lasso.

Daley: Oh, yes. *I wonder why.*

Brianna: He probably expected to scare her and instead, she scared him. You can tell from his face that he is scared of her. He doesn't want to be captured by her.

Daley: That's true. I guess that's why in the next picture he is trying to hide from her and the author writes that he's "crouching down away from her."

Brianna: And in the other book we read, *Amelia Bedelia*, the same thing happens. Amelia Bedelia keeps doing stuff that surprises and confuses Mrs. Rogers.

Daley: Can you show me those parts?

Brianna: Well, when Mrs. Rogers tells her to dust the furniture, she puts white powder all over the furniture.

Daley: Can you say more about that?

Brianna: She saw this box with the words "dusting powder" and thought it was some kind of special powder to dust with.

Daley: So are you saying Mrs. Rogers is like the nightmare?

Brianna: Yes. When she looks around the house and sees all the things Amelia did, like cutting the towels, dressing up the turkey in clothes, and covering the furniture with powder, she is confused. She thought Amelia Bedelia would do things one way, but she did them another way.

Daley: So are you saying that Mrs. Rogers and the nightmare both expected the other character to behave in a certain way and when they don't, they are shocked and surprised?

Conversation continues for several minutes.

Daley: Did anyone notice the kind of talk that Brianna and I were having?

Nicholas: Yeah. Brianna found something that was the same about the characters in the two books.

Daley: That's right—she made a smart connection between our books. She noticed that two of the characters were acting the same way. Let's see if you guys can compare two books you read today and find anything that is the same between the books and we can share them at the end of our workshop. Let's also add this talk strategy to our class chart.

To help students use this technique, I have partners share their text-to-text connections with the class over the next few days. I add to our strategy chart helpful questions to use when thinking about text-to-text connections.

Strategy #4: Make Text-to-Text Connections Between Two Books by Asking: ———

❖ "How are these books the same?"
❖ "Do the characters in one book remind you of the characters in the other book?"
❖ "What is the same about the way the characters act, feel, or think?"

The Strategy in Action
Partner Conversation #1:
Partners are reading the texts Fox at School *and* Fox and His Friends *by Edward Marshall and noticing that the main character, Fox, acts the same way in both texts.*

Partner 1: Fox is not responsible in both books and it causes bad things to happen.

Partner 2: Yeah, in one book he doesn't practice his lines for the class play, which almost ruins the performance.

Partner 1: And in the second book, he doesn't keep an eye on his sister when his mom asks him to baby-sit and then she goes off on her own and almost gets hurt.

Partner 2: And he is lucky because before disaster strikes, both times he gets help from someone else, like his classmate and his mom.

Partner Conversation #2:
Partners are reading the texts Henry and Mudge: The First Book of Their Adventures *and* Mr. Putter and Tabby Pour the Tea *by Cynthia Rylant and comparing how the main characters of each text have similar feelings.*

Partner 1: I noticed that these books are both the first one in each series and the author Cynthia Rylant has the main characters, Henry and Mr. Putter, feeling the same, sad and lonely.

Partner 2: Yeah, and they're both sad because they don't have a best friend. Both of their families are really small. Henry doesn't have any brothers or sisters and Mr. Putter lives by himself.

Partner 1: So they decide to buy a pet, and when they do, their pet becomes their best friend!

Partner 2: Yeah, and the pets, Mudge and Tabby, become part of their family.

◆ MINI-LESSON: EXTENDING BOOK TALK BY MAKING TEXT-WITHIN-TEXT CONNECTIONS ◆

The third type of connection I teach my students to make, text-within-text connections, is the most challenging. Text-within-text connections encourage students to compare and contrast things happening within one text and require readers to examine the text closely to find patterns or themes. Students, for example, may find repeated places in the text where a character feels or acts the same way. Or they may notice how two characters think, act, or feel in similar ways.

I have found that when teaching students to make text-within-text connections it is helpful to have students focus on the characters. I have included a few read-aloud shares from my class where we found text-within-text connections.

To help students use this technique, I add to our strategy chart helpful questions partners can use when thinking about text-within-text connections.

Strategy #5: Make Text-Within-Text Connections by Asking: ————————

❖ "Do any pages show two characters acting the same way? Feeling? Thinking?"
❖ "Does one character act, think, feel the same way over and over?"

The Strategy in Action
Partner Conversation #1:
Before I read aloud Sylvester *and the* Magic Pebble *by William Steig, I ask students to listen and think carefully about how the characters are behaving and feeling in the story. Following the read aloud, partners have a conversation over a copy of the book.*

Partner 1: We noticed that Sylvester and his parents feel the same way at the same time in the book. At the beginning, they are all happy and having a good life.

Partner 2: Sylvester is happy because he found his magic pebble and his parents are happy because they have a great family.

Partner 1: Then in the middle of the story, they all are scared and worried. Sylvester is worried because he is stuck being the rock and his parents are worried because he disappeared and they can't find him.

Partner 2: At the end everyone is happy because everyone is back together.

Partner Conversation #2:

Before I read aloud the text, Wilfrid Gordon McDonald Partridge *by Mem Fox, I ask my students to think about the main characters. Following the read aloud, partners have a conversation about the book and discuss ways the characters are similar in spite of their differences.*

Partner 1: I notice that both Wilfrid and Miss Nancy live with people who take care of them.

Partner 2: Yeah, Wilfrid lives with his parents and Miss Nancy lives with the nurses at the old people's home.

Partner 1: When people are little and old they have to have help taking care of themselves, like eating and getting dressed.

Partner 2: Yeah, babies don't know how to do that stuff and old people sometimes forget to do it or can't 'cause they have trouble moving their body.

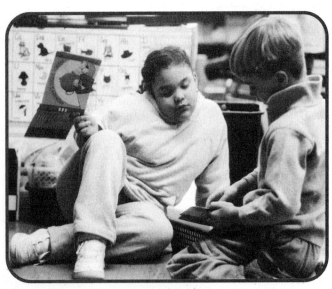

Partners compare and contrast the actions, feelings, and problems of the main characters in the two books they've read together.

Partner Conversation #3:

Same focus as above.

Partner 1: I think that both Wilfrid and Miss Nancy trust each other in the book. That's why they share their secrets and private stuff with each other instead of with everybody else.

Partner 2: I think they trust each other because they spend a lot of time together and become best friends, sort of like a family. Maybe that's why they both have four names.

Partner 1: And even though friends may be different, like a boy and a girl or young and old, they can become best friends, like Wilfrid and Miss Nancy.

Teaching Partners How to Extend Their Book Conversations With Planned Talk

Teaching partners to plan for their talk is the focus of the next unit of study on extending book talk. Planned talk is when partners meet and decide what they will have their conversation about before they read a book. This work includes determining in advance the purpose for their reading, thinking, and talking about books. When you introduce the concept of planned talk and related strategies, explain to students that this practice helps their book conversations stay on track and gives them a choice about what to discuss. I have found that students are eager to make reading plans because they feel a strong sense of empowerment in being given responsibility as well as choices in how they want to decide their reading plans.

The reading plans partners make can vary in format, intensity, and complexity depending on the age level, experience, and reading abilities of your students. Younger students, for example, can choose a text, plan for their talk, read the text together, and talk, all within a single reading partnership session. Older students may meet to choose a text, decide whether they will read the text independently or together, and plan on what they will talk about. In this case, the reading and book-talking may happen over two consecutive partnership sessions. (Typically, older students are fluent readers and don't require support for print work, and therefore read alone. Also, fluent readers often prefer to read independently because silent reading is quicker than oral reading.) If you teach students who are reading lengthier chapter books, explain that partner reading plans need to include a reasonable number of chapters or pages to be read before the partners meet to talk. (In other words, partners meet for book talks regularly no matter the length of their book—they do not wait until they are finished with a chapter book, for example, before talking.)

◆ MINI-LESSON: HOW DO PARTNERS PLAN AHEAD FOR THEIR TALK? ◆

I teach students how partners can preview a text and choose a specific line of thinking that will set the purpose for their reading and talk.

Class gathers on carpet.

Daley: We have been practicing ways to make our book talks interesting and longer. Today we are going to study another strategy that can also help us have great book talks. We are going to plan with our partner what we will talk about before we read a book. When partners decide what they want to talk about before they read a book,

---

How Does Making Reading Plans Benefit Students?

Planning book talks:

◆ builds self-confidence.

◆ encourages decision making.

◆ provides focus for the talk.

◆ fosters independence.

◆ promotes responsibility.

◆ strengthens comprehension skills.

it helps them look for and think about specific ideas while they are reading a book. Who wants to help me show the class how partners can make reading plans?

Sean volunteers to be my partner.

Daley: Sean, why don't we look through your bag of books and first choose a book to read.

We decide to read The Kissing Hand *by Audrey Penn.*

Daley: Let's read the title and look at the cover illustration and think about what we might want to talk about after we read it. There are many things we could talk about so we can think of a few and then pick one we both agree on. For example, we could talk about who our favorite character is and why.

Sean: Or we could try to make a connection between our life and one of the characters.

Daley: That's a great idea. Let's try to make a connection. Let's read this together now and while we are reading, we'll really think about ways the story and characters remind us of ourselves and our lives.

We read the book aloud using the partner reading strategy of taking turns.

Daley: That was a beautiful book. I loved it. The character Chester Raccoon reminded me of myself when I was 5 years old and starting kindergarden. I was scared to go to school, just like Chester. I wanted to stay home with my mom instead of going to school, just like Chester.

Sean: Really? I'm like Chester too, because I used to miss my mom when I went to school. So we thought of a special way that helped me not feel sad when I was away at school like Chester and his mom.

Daley: Did you and your mom do a "kissing hand" like Chester and his mom?

Sean: No, our special way was she wrote me a note every day and put it in my lunch. When I read it during lunch, I knew she was missing me too, and that I would see her soon. It always made me feel better.

Conversation continues for several more minutes with us saying more about our connections between Chester and our own experiences.

Daley: Who noticed something about our book talk?

Supporting Fluent Readers

When a partnership chooses to read a text independently because they are fluent readers, multiple copies of the text need to be available so each partner can have his or her own copy of the text.

The class discusses how we brainstormed possibilities for our talk, chose a focus, had a conversation about our planned focus, and asked each other questions to say more about our personal connection.

Daley: Today you will try to plan what you want to talk about before you read the book with your partner. You can then be gathering ideas for your talk while you read. Remember, there are many things you can talk about. We will be making a list over the next few days of all the different things partners planned to talk about. Go try it!

◆ MINI-LESSON: WHAT CAN PARTNERS PLAN TO TALK ABOUT? ◆

I find it helpful to spend several days having partners share what they chose for their talk focus so that partners will see that there are many possibilities. I use a chart to record the different ways partners plan their talk and encourage my students to try different ways each day.

Class gathers on the carpet.

Daley: Over the past few days, you have been doing amazing talk with your reading partners. I think it is really helping you to plan ahead for your book talks. I noticed many partnerships were talking about different things. I thought it would be helpful if we brainstormed a list of things we have focused our talk on, so that partners can see all the possibilities.

Partners share the different ways they have been talking and I record them on a chart titled "What Can Partners Plan to Talk About?" I list the options partners may choose from simplest to most sophisticated. As I notice that partners have mastered one way to plan, I encourage them to try other possibilities. I use partner conference time to give this feedback.

For the next few days, my mini-lessons are focused on modeling a variety of ways partners can plan ahead for their talk as listed on the chart.

> What Can Partners Plan To Talk About?
> - A favorite page and why?
> - A favorite character and why?
> - A favorite part and why?
> - A confusing part.
> - A surprising part.
> - Something that reminds the reader of their life.
> - Something that reminds the reader of another book.
> - A character's feelings, motivations, actions.
> - Changes in a character and why?

Partners share aloud the different ways they have been talking. These compiled strategies become a resource for partners who may need ideas for planning their talk.

Assessing Students

You can use partner-planning-talk recording sheets to assess the talk strategies students may or may not be using. This data can be helpful when conferring with students and planning upcoming mini-lessons.

To encourage reading partners to vary the focus of their book talks, I introduce a simple recording sheet that holds them accountable for their reading plans. The recording sheet helps me assess (1) what kinds of books partners are choosing to read, (2) how much partners are reading, and (3) what types of conversations partners are having. (A reproducible of the recording sheet is included on page 62.)

Class gathers on the carpet.

Daley: We have been doing some smart planning with our reading partners. We have discovered many ways we can focus our reading even before we start talking, in order to make our book talks really great. Today I am going to show you how we are going to keep track of our partnership reading plans.

A chart-sized version of the recording sheet below is displayed in front of the class.

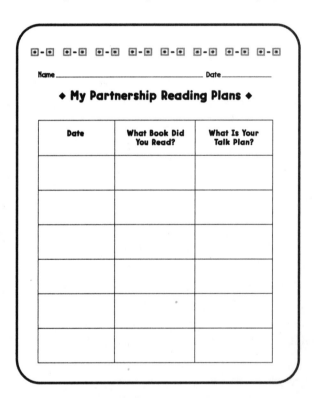

Daley: On this chart I am going to demonstrate how you and your partner record your work each day. Who wants to be my partner today?

Max volunteers to be my partner.

Daley: Max, why don't we look through your bag of books and decide which book we want to read.

We decide to read Swimmy *by Robert Kraus.*

Daley: Let's read the title, look at the cover illustration, and think about what we want to talk about after we read it. There are many things we could talk about, so let's brainstorm a few. We can look at our class chart "What Can Partners Plan to Talk About?" to remind us of some ideas.

Max: Why don't we talk about a character who changes in the story?

Daley: Great. We can see if a character is one way at the beginning of the story and then different at the end because of something that happens in the story. We'll try to find out what causes the character to change. Let's record our reading plan before we read.

I fill in the date, title, and talk plan on the chart.

Daley: Now let's read the book and be thinking about and noticing characters who change during the story and try to figure out how they change and why.

I continue the mini-lesson by reading the book with Max and then engaging in a conversation about a main character who changed during the story.

Over the course of the next few mini-lessons, I model how partners plan ahead and record their talk plan. For instance, a partnership reading a text with two main characters, such as Frog and Toad (Arnold Lobel) or Pinky and Rex (James Howe) may decide to discuss ways in which the characters are alike and different. On the other hand, a partnership of struggling readers who may be reading a C- or D-level book may focus on noticing how the illustrations add to the story that the words tell.

Name _____ Date _____

◆ My Partnership Reading Plans ◆

Date	What Book Did You Read?	What Is Your Talk Plan?
January 22	Swimmy	A character change

When partnerships meet each day, I remind them to begin by quickly filling in their planning sheet. For management ease, they keep this sheet in their book bags. I collect them at the end of each week and use them to plan for follow-up instruction.

Name_____ Date_____

◆ My Partnership Reading Plans ◆

Date	What Book Did You Read?	What Is Your Talk Plan?

◆ **MINI-LESSON: USING STICKY NOTES TO PREPARE FOR BOOK TALKS** ◆

As part of planning for partner talk, I also teach students to use sticky notes to help them get ready for their book conversation. I teach them that sticky notes can be used to mark pages in the book that are related to their planned talk topic. Some students find it helpful to attach sticky notes as they are reading a text and noticing how specific words or illustrations support their planned conversation. Other students will prefer to first read the text (or chapters) entirely and then review the pages and attach sticky notes where appropriate. The use and placement of sticky notes helps students gather, organize, and plan the ideas they will share. During conversations, the sticky notes serve as a tool for building purposeful and focused book talks.

Effective use of sticky notes requires explicit instruction and modeling. In fact, I spend several mini-lessons teaching students how and when to use sticky notes with the texts they read. As students become competent using sticky notes, I also teach them how to record their thinking on the sticky notes.

Class gathers on carpet.

Daley: We have been practicing using sticky notes with our guided reading texts and I think we are ready to use them now in our partnerships. We are going to use the sticky notes to mark the pages of the text that have words and pictures that will help our books talks. Who would like to help me demonstrate this strategy?

Teaching Students to Use Sticky Notes

◆ Use small group settings, like guided reading, to provide students with frequent support for and practice of sticky notes usage.

◆ Give students a small number of sticky notes to use with a text, to prevent random use or overuse of sticky notes.

PURPOSES OF TEACHING STUDENTS TO USE STICKY NOTES

◆ Motivates partners to prepare for their talk.
◆ Organizes partners' thinking.
◆ Encourages partners to look closely at words and illustrations and highlight those that relate to the intended talk topic.
◆ Allows partners to work independently, reading and gathering ideas for an upcoming talk session.
◆ Serves as a resource partners can refer to during book talk.
◆ Provides teachers with a way to assess partnerships.

Assessing Partners' Use of Sticky Notes

Teachers can use, in conjunction with students' partner planning sheets, the sticky notes students place and record on in their texts. This strategy shows whether students are able to find places in the text that (1) support their thinking and (2) relate to the planned book-talk topic.

Siobhan volunteers to be my partner. Siobhan and I select Frog and Toad Are Friends *by Arnold Lobel. We decide to read and notice if the characters behave differently from each other. After reading the text, we discuss how Toad often behaves like a child and Frog often behaves like an adult. We placed sticky notes on pages of the text that supported our idea.*

Siobhan: I put a sticky note on page seven because it said that Toad wouldn't get out of bed when Frog was trying to wake him up in the morning, just like a mom or dad has to do in the morning for their kids. But Toad kept hiding under his covers because he wanted to sleep all day, which is what kids do a lot in the morning.

Daley: Great! That was a smart idea for a sticky note because the words and pictures on that page were evidence for our idea that Frog is like a parent and Toad is like a child. I put a sticky note on page 36 because the picture shows Toad throwing a temper tantrum like a baby, because he can't find his button. I also wrote on the sticky note the words the author used to show his behavior, "He jumped up and down and screamed," because it's proof for our idea.

The conversation continues, showing that Siobhan and I are using this tool to help us keep track of the idea we are formulating.

◆ MINI-LESSON: CROSS-PARTNERSHIP SHARES USING STICKY NOTES ◆

I spend several mini-lessons having pairs of partnerships work together. Each partnership demonstrates their use of sticky notes during their talk. The observing partners are expected to provide feedback and helpful criticism to strengthen the other partnership's use of sticky notes. These experiences also help students understand that sticky notes are extremely helpful when a book talk takes place on a later day because they are a "permanent" record of the partnership's thinking and talking about a specific idea.

◆ MINI-LESSON: WHAT ARE WAYS STICKY NOTES CAN BE USED TO FOCUS BOOK TALKS? ◆

When partners are planning ahead for their talk, there are many ways they can decide to focus their conversation and use sticky notes: from very simple to more complex. I explain to students that many of the possibilities for talk listed on the class chart "What Can Partners Plan to Talk About?" are also ways for partners to use sticky notes. I spend several mini-lessons teaching various uses of sticky notes. Over the course of the mini-lessons, I make a class chart that outlines ways sticky notes are used.

I have partnerships who used sticky notes in different ways share with the class their work. Here are two excerpts of partnerships using sticky notes.

The Strategy in Action
Partner Conversation #1:
Partners are reading and making connections between two texts in the Commander Toad series by Jane Yolen.

Partner 1: In both books, the author makes jokes by changing real words to funny frog words. In the book *Commander Toad and the Voyage Home*, we put a sticky note on page eight and wrote the author's words "the ship is called Star Warts," which she used instead of writing "Star Wars." And we also put a sticky note on page 32 and wrote the author's words, "Then they hop out of the skimmer and stand shoulder to shoulder in a toadal circle" instead of a "total" circle.

Partner 2: In the other book, *Commander Toad and the Planet of the Grapes*, we found lots of frog-word jokes too. We put a sticky note on page 14, which said the crew's favorite song was "Hoppy Birthday" instead of "Happy Birthday." And on page 13, the picture shows the crew's chess set has different kinds of frogs wearing space outfits instead of the regular pieces and outfits, so we put a sticky note there.

Partnership Conversation #2:
Partners are reading and talking about how a character behaves in different ways in the text Fox at School *by Edward Marshall.*

Partner 1: We had the idea that Fox sometimes acts very responsible and mature and sometimes he acts really silly and immature. So we put some sticky notes on pages that showed him acting both ways. On page 13, we wrote on our sticky note that "he was being immature when he wasn't practicing his lines for the class play." And on page 43, we put a sticky note on the picture because it shows Fox letting all the kids in his class go crazy when his teacher leaves him in charge for a few minutes. We wrote on the sticky note that "the kids are making faces, throwing airplanes, and standing on the desks."

> **In What Ways Can Sticky Notes Be Used to Mark Pages for Our Book Talks?**
>
> Sticky notes can highlight:
> - a favorite page or part,
> - a favorite character,
> - a confusing part,
> - a connection,
> - a change in character behavior,
> - an idea about a character,
> - author's or illustrator's style.

Partner 2: We put a sticky note on page 30 because it shows him acting the opposite way. It's when he tells his teacher the truth that he is afraid to go down the slide during the school fire drill. When he is being honest like that, it's mature behavior. And also on page 48 he is mature because he gets the class to calm down and start reading by the time his teacher, Miss Moon, gets back.

As partners become competent using sticky notes to prepare for their talk, they start to record their thinking on them as well, because they see how it helps during the talk. I add "What can we write on the sticky notes?" to our class chart as students practice and share their work with sticky notes.

Writing Notes to Save Time

I encourage students to write a few words or short phrases on sticky notes rather than spending time writing lengthy sentences. This way, the majority of their partner time is spent reading and talking about their ideas rather than on writing.

We can use sticky notes to mark pages for:	What can we write on the sticky notes?
a special page or part	What makes it special? How does it help the story?
a favorite character	Who is it? Why is that character your favorite?
a confusing part	What is confusing: a word? an idea?
a connection	How does it remind you of your life? How does it remind you of another book? Another character?
a change in character behavior	How and why does the character change during the story?
an idea about a character	What evidence supports your idea?
author's or illustrator's style	What is special or unique about the words, ideas, pictures, or text?

Helping students become active decision makers and self-motivated readers who plan is an important goal in the teaching of reading. Partnership work can help students achieve this goal by providing daily opportunities for partners to practice a repertoire of strategies. This gives them flexibility and choices in deciding what they will read, think, and talk about. Chapters 5 and 6 further explore how you can structure partner work to deepen students' comprehension of and engagement with texts through reading centers.

Chapter 5

Growing Partnerships in Reading Centers

Brian and Ashley, second-grade reading partners, are discussing and adding to their prior knowledge of penguins by reading and comparing several nonfiction books as part of a class nonfiction reading center study. (The second-grade science curriculum focuses on the concept of life cycles.)

Brian: I notice in the picture that when penguins are born, their skin isn't the black smooth kind. It says in the caption below the picture that they have brown downy feathers on the outside of their bodies when they are first born. I wonder what happens to those furry feathers?

Ashley: It says here that the feathers are the reason the babies can't go into the water to swim and catch food. If they went in the water with their furry skin, they would get really cold and sick because the fur wouldn't keep their body warm enough. It doesn't say what happens to the feathers, though.

The partners read a few pages of another text.

Brian: Here it is. It says they shed the brown furry feathers. Their body makes them fall off automatically. And underneath the furry feathers is their black smooth skin that we usually see in pictures of penguins.

Ashley: Yeah, it's like they're shedding their fur. Some other animals shed their fur too, like my cat every spring.

Brian: It says that after the penguins shed their feathers they can go in the water and won't freeze or get sick. Their black skin is like a wet suit. It's like divers who can go in really cold water for a long time and don't get cold or sick because their wet suit protects their body.

This chapter shows how primary students can engage in book conversations about complex concepts similar to the one captured above, by working in a kind of reading partnership called reading centers.

What Are Reading Centers?

Reading centers resemble study groups or book clubs in that they are initiated by teachers and students. Reading centers encourage small groups of students to read a collection of texts that are related. The collection of books students read can be connected by topic, genre, or concept. Students work in partnerships during reading centers. While partners read texts, they gather information and make sense of it by talking to one another about the material they've read. Practices of reading centers motivate students to read, make inferences, draw conclusions, and discuss their thoughts through conversation.

Reading center studies in your classroom can develop from students' interest in a particular topic, genre, or concept, and from your assessment of students' needs. The widespread choices you have in choosing the focus of each reading center study allows you the flexibility to integrate this structure into your reading program throughout the school year.

In my classroom, for example, I have students participate in five to eight reading center studies throughout the year. Typically, I organize reading center studies that reflect the genres we are studying in reading and writing (nonfiction and poetry) or the concepts we are studying in science and social studies (e.g., insect metamorphosis and community). The books I choose for the study are related to the specific focus.

During a nonfiction reading center study, for instance, the baskets I put together might each contain a set of nonfiction books about insects. Each basket would have books all about one kind of insect, representing a variety of reading levels. The baskets would also have other materials the students use for their reading center work, including sticky notes and center activity sheets.

What Are the Benefits of Reading Centers?

Some of the benefits that reading centers provide to students and teachers include:

♦ Reading centers encourage students to read and reread texts.
♦ Reading centers allow students to work on books at their reading level but be exposed to books on other levels as well.
♦ Reading centers can support, build on, and extend partner work.
♦ Reading centers allow students at different reading levels to work together.
♦ Reading centers introduce students to genres, concepts, topics, and specific aspects of reading.
♦ Reading centers provide for effective mini-lessons because every partnership is involved in reading the same kinds of texts.
♦ Reading centers encourage thoughtful book talk that helps students gain a deeper understanding of what they read.
♦ Reading centers offer opportunities for students to compare and contrast texts, one of the basic literacy standards.

(Source: Elizabeth Phillips, P.S. 321 principal)

How Are Partners Grouped in a Reading Center?

I have found it helpful to have four students share the books in a reading center basket. In this way, each group of four students can be subdivided into two partnerships. I usually designate a specific area of the classroom for each reading center basket. (Therefore, on reading center days, students are able to get their basket, move to their location, and begin working in an efficient and timely manner.) At each reading center area, the two partnerships sit apart, so their reading and talking are not distracting to one another.

The partnerships created for reading centers are usually different from daily reading partnerships. (I have found that my students enjoy having opportunities to work with different reading partners.) In reading centers, unlike reading partnerships, partnerships can but don't have to be ability based. In this way, you have the flexibility of using heterogeneous or homogeneous partnerships for reading center studies.

My decision to partner students by ability or group them by their interest in a topic is determined by the study focus as well as the books I collect. During our nonfiction study, for example, my purpose is to have students explore and understand the style and conventions of these texts. I fill each basket with books that span many reading levels. Because partners can talk and discover ideas about their subject by studying the pictures

Value and Purposes of Reading Centers

♦ Students work in partnerships.
♦ Students read actively.
♦ Students engage in book talks.
♦ Students work on a specific line of thinking, toward a "big idea" about their book.

(Source: Kathy Collins, Teachers College Reading and Writing Project, Columbia University)

and structures of the texts (e.g., captions, table of contents, boldfaced vocabulary words), the work required of students is not dependent on their ability to read each text in its entirety. Therefore, in this study, I don't need to group students in ability-based partnerships. Instead, I use the opportunity to create partnerships based on student interest in the nonfiction topics.

When I have students participate in character reading centers, however, I have them work in ability-based partnerships. This makes sense, because each basket contains books on one character (e.g., Clifford, Amelia Bedelia, Biscuit) and all of the books in a series are usually written on a similar reading level. It is therefore helpful that both partners are able to read the books in their baskets.

What Do Reading Center Partners Do?

Like daily reading partnerships, reading center partners read and talk about books. One difference is that because the books in reading centers are connected by topic, concept, or genre of the center study, partners are able to compare and contrast the texts read and gradually develop big ideas about the topic, genre, or concept.

In my classroom, I use the terms *hunch* and *big idea* during reading center studies when I explain to students the work they will be engaging in and focusing their partner talk around. As partners read their collection of related texts and compare them, they develop hunches. Partners keep these hunches—what we call their "specific line of thinking"—in mind when they read. As they read new books each day, partners learn information that requires them to revise their hunches. At the conclusion of the reading center study, partnerships have, as a result of their reading and talking, gathered evidence from multiple texts that support their hunch, which now becomes a big idea. In our ABC study, for example, one partnership's big idea at the end of the study was that all alphabet books begin with the letter *a*. For first graders this idea was a huge discovery and was proved by comparing the first page of each text read.

During a whole-class reading center study, mini-lessons are used to teach students how to compare texts, develop hunches, and prove big ideas. The mini-lessons that support reading centers are incredibly effective because they directly apply to your entire class—all students are reading the same type of texts. (Later in the chapter an outline of suggested reading center mini-lessons is provided for teaching students how to compare texts and develop big ideas.)

When Can You Implement Reading Centers?

Reading centers can take place at various times throughout the school year to support your curriculum and students' reading needs. I usually have a cycle of reading centers every six weeks. My decision to engage my students in a reading center study is based on the requirements of the reading, writing, social studies, and science curricula and what students are struggling with most in their reading work. (Chapter 6 provides a sample calendar of my reading centers throughout the year.)

The ABC study is my first reading center study each year. It is geared toward teaching the early concepts of reading, including letter-sound knowledge, beginning book concepts (e.g., parts of books, print directionality), and print strategies (e.g., matching pictures to words). The ABC texts provide practice and review of these reading readiness skills through context rather than in isolation. Students are incredibly excited to work with these fascinating texts and feel proud to be working with actual books, especially ones that they are not reading for independent or guided reading. (Chapter 6 describes in depth an ABC reading center study.)

Reading centers also make a great complement for our writing studies. When teaching genres of writing such as poetry, nonfiction, and fiction, I have found it extremely helpful to have my students engage in reading centers studying these types of texts in depth. A month before beginning a unit of study in writing on nonfiction, for example, I have my students participate in reading centers on nonfiction texts. As partners read, compare, and talk about nonfiction books, they discover the conventions, styles, and formats of nonfiction texts. As a result of the intensive reading center work my students engage in, they are successful in writing nonfiction pieces, using many of the conventions studied in their reading centers (e.g., table of contents, captions, and glossaries).

I have even developed reading centers to focus on key reading standards such as fluency. I call these "reading centers that help us read better."

How Do Reading Center Partnerships Compare With Daily Reading Partnerships and Support Your Reading Program?

When my class is engaged in a reading center study, my reading program includes both daily reading partnerships and reading center partnerships. Within the two-to-three-week reading center study, for example, I alternate between the two practices each day. In a given week, for instance, I have three days of reading center partnerships and two days of daily reading partnerships. In this way, I use each to support the skills and concepts of the curriculum.

Both types of partnerships serve specific purposes in a reading program. The points below show how a reading program that incorporates both daily reading partnerships and reading center partnerships supports students' different learning needs as they acquire reading skills and better understand curriculum concepts. Kathy Collins explores these ideas further in *Growing Readers: Units of Study in the Primary Classroom* (2004).

Grouping: Reading center partnerships are sometimes interest based, whereas reading partnerships are always ability based. (See ideas for interest-based reading centers on pages 73–75.)

Reading level: Partners always read at level in ability-based reading partnerships, allowing them to practice a specific print strategy (using chunks in words), reading strategy (using punctuation to guide expression), or reading comprehension strategy (retelling across five fingers) with the help of their partner and appropriately leveled texts. The range of leveled reading materials available in reading centers, however, may require partners to "read" above or below their level for other purposes. For example, the levels of ABC book texts vary quite a bit, from one word on a page to dense paragraphs of information on a featured object. Partners working with an ABC reading center have a chance to sample a variety of formats within the ABC genre and compare and contrast different text structures.

Partners read "across" a set of Frog and Toad books in a character reading center study

Number and type of texts read: Usually, in daily reading partnerships, partners focus on a single book and study it with a specific focus. From their at-level book bags, they choose books that vary in topic and genre. In this way, partners are able to practice the reading skills and strategies taught during the mini-lessons with texts at their specific reading level. Reading centers provide students with the opportunity to read and practice strategies across a set of similar texts. Reading a group of books that are similar in topic, genre, or concept motivates student to look across the books, comparing and contrasting the texts and developing hunches about the unit of study which may lead them to form big ideas (hunches that have been proved across many books).

Shared learning objectives: In daily reading partnerships, partners focus on reading skills that match their specific learning needs. In reading centers, several partners or the whole class can read books and follow specific lines of thinking related to these texts, such as concepts about weather or life cycles.

What Are Some Suggested Topics for Reading Centers?

Reading centers can be used to introduce, explore, and learn about a particular genre, kind of book, or aspect of reading. Here are some ideas I've used for reading center studies. (An example of a study topic with a list of recommended titles is included for each category of reading center study.)

──────────────── ◆ CONCEPT STUDIES ◆ ────────────────

📖 pattern books

📖 list books

📖 alphabet books

📖 wordless books

📖 number books

📖 family books

📖 holiday books

📖 birthday books

📖 rhyming books

📖 friendship books

📖 feelings books

📖 song books

📖 big books

📖 class books

◆ A FRIENDSHIP READING CENTER STUDY, GRADES 1–3 ◆

Emergent Readers, Guided Reading Levels A–D:

My Friend at School by Patricia Cousin et al.

Going to the Park With Granddaddy by Patricia Cousin et al.

Bo and Peter by Betsy Franco

My Monster by Nana Kijak

Friends by Martin Meyer

See What I Can Do! by Mary Pearson

My Best Friend by Deborah Sycamore

We Are Friends by Mara Vasquez

Early Readers, Guided Reading Levels E–I

Biscuit by Alyssa Satin Capucilli

A Rainbow of Friends by P. K. Hallinan

Best Friends by Cass Hollander

First Grade Friends (series) by Grace Maccarone

Best Friends in the Snow by Angela Medearis

The Friendship Garden by Angela Medearis

My Friend Jess by Diana Noonan

A Friend for Max by Annette Smith

Fluent Readers, Guided Reading Levels J–L

PeeWee Scouts (series) by Judy Delton

Penny and Pup by Linda Jennings

Danny and the Dinosaur (series) by Syd Hoff

Jake and Rosie by Patricia Lillie

Little Bear (series) by Else Holmelund Minarik

Mr. Putter (series) by Cynthia Rylant

Henry and Mudge (series) by Cynthia Rylant

M and M (series) by Pat Ross

◆ GENRE STUDIES ◆

- 📖 mysteries
- 📖 nonfiction
- 📖 poetry
- 📖 biography
- 📖 fairy tales/folktales

- 📖 magazines
- 📖 comics
- 📖 recipes
- 📖 manuals

◆ A NONFICTION READING CENTER STUDY, GRADES 1–3 ◆

Mixed Guided Reading Levels (Series)

Concept Science: Animals, Modern Curriculum Press
Eyewitness Junior, Dorling Kindersley
First Discovery Books, Scholastic
I Can Read About, Troll
Let's Read and Find Out, Harper Collins
Literacy 2000, Rigby
Look Closer, Dorling Kindersley
My World Books, Steck-Vaughn
Read All About It, Steck-Vaughn
Rookies Read About Science, Children's Press
Science, Zaner-Bloser

Sunshine Science Books, Wright Group
Time-to-Discover, Scholastic
Twig Books, Wright Group
Wonder World III, Wright Group

Nonfiction Magazines

Click, Carus Publishing
Cricket, Carus Publishing
Ladybug, Carus Publishing
Ranger Rick, National Wildlife Federation
Spider, Carus Publishing
Time for Kids, Time Publications

Book baskets for
a nonfiction study
on plants.

◆ **OTHER STUDIES** ◆ ─────────

📖 **character study**

📖 **author study**

📖 **series**

📖 **story elements**

📖 **interest**

📖 **favorite books**

📖 **read alouds**

◆ A CHARACTER READING CENTER STUDY, GRADES 1–3 ◆

Emergent Readers, Guided Reading Levels A–E

Maisy (series) by Lucy Cousins

Huggles (series) by Joy Cowley

Mrs. Wishy-Washy by Joy Cowley

Pig, Worm, Monkey, Tabby Cat, Ruby the Sheep, Dinah the Dinosaur, Winnie the Dog, Brand New Reader (series) by David Martin, B. G. Hennessy, et al.

Tiny by Cari Meister

Early Readers, Guided Reading Levels F–I

Biscuit (series) by Allyssa Satin Capucilli

Danny the Dinosaur (series) by Syd Hoff

Titch (series) by Pat Hutchins

Dragon (series) by Dav Pilkey

Baby Bear (series) by Beverley Randell

Harry the Hippo (series) by Harriet Ziefert

Fluent Readers, Guided Reading Levels J–N

Cam Jansen (series) by David A. Adler

Julian (series) by Ann Cameron

Jenny Archer (series) by Ellen Conford

Aunt Eater (series) by Doug Cushman

Jamaica (series) by Juanita Havill

Pinky and Rex (series) by James Howe

Peter (series) by Erza Jack Keats

Horrible Harry (series) by Suzy Kline

Junie B. Jones (series) by Barbara Park

M and M (series) by Pat Ross

Poppleton (series) by Cynthia Rylant

Oliver and Amanda Pig (series) by Jean Van Leeuwen

Fluent Readers, Guided Reading Levels O–W

My Teacher . . . by Bruce Coville

Bunnicula by Deborah Howe and James Howe

Orphan Train Adventures (series) by Joan Lowery Nixon

Amos Gets (series) by Gary Paulsen

Time Warp Trio (series) by Jon Scieszka

Dragon Cauldron and others by Lawrence Yep

Getting Partners Ready to Work in Reading Centers

ollowing are tips to help you prepare students for partner work in reading centers.

Establish daily reading partnerships: For reading centers to work effectively, it is important that your students have experience working in reading partnerships. Students should be able to read books with a partner and discuss in meaningful and purposeful ways what they have read. The management, routines, and expectations you have established for daily reading partnerships, therefore, will be easily transferred to partner work in reading centers. (Chapter 3 focuses on organizing and managing daily partnerships.)

Choose a topic: You can decide on a reading center study topic based on your curriculum as well as the interests and needs of your students.

Select books: When you choose books for centers, consider the content, quality, and reading level of the texts. For struggling and early readers, for example, it is helpful to choose books with strong picture support and simple text.

To build student enthusiasm for an upcoming study of reading centers, involve students in the selection of books for the centers. The students can, for instance, search the classroom library as well as their homes for books that can be added to the center baskets.

When creating baskets of books for reading centers, I spend a lot of time thinking about book levels. For a center study on character, for instance, each basket serves a particular reading level of my students.
A basket of Frog and Toad books, for example, serves my fluent readers while a basket of Huggles books serves my emergent readers. When I do centers on nonfiction, however, I group books in baskets by topic. In each nonfiction basket, I make sure to include books at the emergent, early, and fluent levels to meet the needs of my students.

Immerse students in the topic: Several weeks before beginning a cycle of reading centers, create an air of excitement and enthusiasm about the upcoming reading centers by reading aloud books that are related to the center study. (These books can be put in the reading center baskets so that partners have the option of working with familiar texts you have read.)

For some studies such as our friendship study, I might choose one text to be a touchstone text (*source: Teachers College Reading and Writing Project, Columbia University*). A touchstone text is one that you read aloud repeatedly to your students and include in each reading center basket, if multiple copies are available. With each rereading of the touchstone text, students are able to notice new things. This repeated read-aloud strategy enables you to guide the book talk beyond the literal meaning of the text. (Chapter 4 describes ways teachers model and teach students to engage in deep and meaningful book conversations.) I have found that by working with one text in a concentrated manner, students are able to think deeply about the text. The talk practices you model during these repeated readings are ones students can transfer to their partner conversations—and students feel empowered to use this familiar text to make comparisons with the other texts in their reading center basket.

> ### Choosing Touchstone Texts
>
> A touchstone text is one with:
>
> ◆ an engaging text,
>
> ◆ unique and interesting illustrations,
>
> ◆ multiple copies available.

What Does a Typical Reading Center Study Look Like?

◆ THE LAUNCH ◆

Days 1 and 2 : Exploring days

Once the reading center books have been collected and sorted into the baskets, I have students preview the books in each basket before choosing the basket they will work with during the study. Over the course of two days, during our daily partner reading time, my students work in small groups exploring the books in each basket. I usually allow groups about five minutes to preview each basket.

When students are previewing books, I ask them to consider whether the books are of interest to them as well as whether the books are close to their reading level ("just right" books). To preview books, I encourage students to read the title, take a picture walk, and read the first few pages of the text. Using this technique, students determine if a basket of books is too easy, too hard, or just right. (Chapter 2 describes how students learn to choose "just right" books.)

Character study baskets hold about six to eight books—more for struggling readers because their books are shorter.

Day 3: Choosing baskets and partners

After students explore the baskets of books, I display a chart listing the names of the center baskets. On each basket I have an index card indicating the basket's name. For our character study, for example, I use the character names to label the baskets. For our ABC study, I identify baskets by color since they are all labeled "ABC books."

As I read the name of each basket, students who want to work with those books raise their hand. By having students select centers in this manner, they feel empowered and part of the decision-making process, while I am still able to choose the students who will work best with each basket of books. If, for example, I have a student who volunteers for the Henry and Mudge character reading center and that student is an emergent reader, I will not choose that student but rather choose four volunteers who are fluent readers. (Most students are able to determine "just right" reading center baskets because of the earlier instruction on distinguishing between books that are too hard, too easy, and just right, and they therefore volunteer for appropriate book baskets.)

As I choose volunteers for each center, students print their names on the chart. I always try to have an even number of students (two or four) for each basket. Once each student has chosen a center, the students gather at their reading center location, which I've determined, and divide into partnerships of two. I remind students to be considerate of one another's feelings when choosing partners and to consider who will be a cooperative partner. (Chapter 3 includes mini-lessons on teaching students how to be a "good partner.")

The newly formed partnerships spend the remaining time sketching the covers of their center packets, which contain written work such as graphic organizers that the partners will complete during the study. Center packet materials serve as a record of the partners' thinking and growth during our study and provide assessment materials for parent conferences. (Chapter 6 includes sample reproducibles for an ABC study center packet.)

During a study on character, students sketch and color a picture of their character on the center packet cover.

◆ THE MINI-LESSONS ◆

I usually spend six to seven days on a reading center study over the course of two weeks. As described on page 71, I schedule reading centers every other day, during our partner reading time.
On reading center days, my reading workshop mini-lesson focuses on the center work partners will be engaged in. The following is an outline of mini-lessons for a center study. (Chapter 6 provides mini-lessons for one specific study, an ABC study, as well as examples of the student work described below.)

Day 1: What book will you read?
On the first day of reading centers, I explain to students that each day partners will choose one book to read and talk about. I encourage partners to read the books using a variety of their strategies (e.g., echoing, taking turns chorally). During the mini-lesson, the class brainstorms ways partners can decide who gets to choose the new book each day (e.g., taking turns each day) and how the book can be read best (e.g., an ABC riddle book can be read with one partner reading the clues and one partner guessing the answer). I usually have a partnership role-play these practices for the whole class before sending students off to work in their centers.

While students are engaged in their reading centers each day, I observe and confer with partnerships. (Later in the chapter, I outline ways teachers can support and guide the talk between partners while conferring.) When conferring with partnerships, I make sure to first observe their work and use this "research" to decide what to teach. In this way, my teaching reflects the needs of each partnership. I also use my conferences to identify partnerships that can model the practices I've taught during the mini-lessons. For example, during a character reading center study, I might choose a partnership that reads their Frog and Toad text by having each partner read the words of one of the characters as a way to demonstrate interesting ways partners can read texts.

Day 2: What are you noticing?
I begin the mini-lesson by showing the class two books we have previously read aloud and discussed. (These books are related to the reading center topic and are in my center basket.) I begin asking questions that encourage students to compare these two texts and notice similarities and differences. (Chapter 4 describes ways students can learn to make connections between texts and ask one another prompting questions.)

I explain to my class that their reading center work that day will be to choose a second book to read. While the partners are reading their second book, they should keep in mind the first book they read. After

Partnerships With Fluent Readers

Fluent reading partners may decide to read the entire book or an agreed-upon number of chapters independently and come together for the talk. To support this practice, you will need multiple copies of each book title. Chapter 4 describes how fluent partners can meet, make reading plans, read independently, and come together for their book talk.

partners finish reading the second book, they can begin to compare the two books to see if they notice any things that are the same about the texts. (For example, partners participating in centers on fairy tales might notice that both of their fairy-tale books begin and end in similar ways.) When students engage in this type of work for the first time, what they notice may appear small or obvious. But through practice and experience, they will successfully push their thinking and discover deeper meanings.

You have the option to make the work that students engage in on the second day more or less open-ended. For example, during a nonfiction study, you may use the mini-lesson to explicitly teach students to look at one of the conventions of the texts (e.g., table of contents, glossary). Or you may make the mini-lesson less explicit to see what students will discover by themselves.

During the share part of the workshop, I choose several partners to share what they notice about the books they have read. I encourage each partnership to show the class the pages in the books that they are comparing and describing. For example, a partnership noticing that the two fairy-tale texts they read began and ended the same way would show and read the supporting text to the class. During this share time, I introduce my students to the term *hunch* to describe the similarities partners are noticing when comparing books they've read. I might say, for instance, "So, the hunch you are developing about fairy-tale books is that they begin and end in the same way. And you are using the pictures and words of the texts to support your hunch." I encourage students to keep their hunches in mind for the following day's reading center work.

Day 3: What hunches are you gathering? Are you revising your hunches as you read more?

I explain to students that they will choose another book to read, keeping in mind their hunch or hunches from the previous sessions. After partners read the third book, they will consider and discuss, "Does this new book fit with the hunch we came up with previously? Does this book have words and/or pictures to support our hunch?" For example, during our character study, the class had an initial hunch about the characters Frog and Toad, which were the books in my teaching basket. After comparing the first two books, the class had a hunch that Frog was always a helpful, kind friend while toad was typically lazy and grumpy. However, after listening and comparing the chapter "The Swim," in which Toad asks Frog not to laugh when he sees him wearing his bathing suit because he is embarrassed by it and Frog agrees but then does laugh along with the other animals when he sees Toad in his suit, the class decided to change, or revise, their initial hunch. On a sticky note, I

recorded the class hunch "Frog is usually the kinder, more mature friend and Toad is usually the immature, lazy one" and placed it on the class chart titled, "What Hunches Are We Gathering About Our Characters?" (For each center study, I have a class chart titled, "What Hunches Are You Gathering About Our _____ Books?") I emphasize to students that often a hunch will need to be changed as they read more books. I also use the term *revise*, which is familiar to my students from our writing process work, to describe how readers, like writers, continuously make changes as they are working on a piece or reading a text.

During the workshop share, I read aloud the hunches partners have gathered and recorded on the sticky notes. I am careful to refrain from commenting whether a hunch may later be modified or disproved because I want partners to come to this realization as they continue to read, compare, and talk about their books. For example, one of my partnerships reading alphabet books during our ABC study proposed that every "e" page in an alphabet book has an illustration of an egg. The partnership had read three alphabet books, all of which had an egg on the "e" page. As they continued the study, they read books with different illustrations on the "e" page and realized that their hunch was not true for all ABC books. I left the discovery to them. Later I encouraged them to change their hunch to read "Many ABC books have eggs on the 'e' page."

It is also expected during the share time that one partnership may disagree or debate the validity of a recorded hunch. Disagreeing and debating ideas is a welcome practice in my classroom. (Chapter 4 describes ways teachers can foster debate between students in a respectful way.) When a partnership disagrees with another partnership's hunch, I encourage them to get a book they have read that will provide proof as to why they are questioning the proposed hunch. Other times, I will say, "Well, it seems like some people disagree. I think we should keep reading more books with our partner today and discover if this hunch needs to be revised."

Partners begin to develop hunches about a character by comparing the character across a book series.

Day 4: What hunches can be proved? Disproved?
For the mini-lesson, I review the meaning of the word *disprove*. I write on the bottom half of our chart, "What hunches are we gathering about our _____ texts?" and "What hunches have we disproved?"

I explain to students that they will be choosing a fourth book to read from their basket. As they read it, they should keep in mind their hunches and gather the evidence to prove or disprove their hunch.

During the center session, I encourage students to change the hunches they recorded on sticky notes. Students may change a statement of "all" to "some," "many," "often," or "usually" and keep the hunch in the "proved" section of the chart. Others will move the sticky note to the "disproved" section of the chart. I usually include an activity sheet in the student reading center packets where they also record their hunches at the end of this session. (Chapter 6 provides an example of this activity sheet. See page 106.)

For the share part of the workshop, partnerships tell the class about the hunches they have developed and can support with evidence from each text they have read. I use the term *big idea* to describe the hunches that are proven across a series of texts.

Day 5: What text will you reread?
Before the mini-lesson, I ask partners to look over the books they have read and consider whether they want to reread a text or read a new one during that session.

For the mini-lesson, I ask a few partnerships to share why they want to reread a text from their basket. Some partners may want to reread a book because they want to reread it using a different reading technique, while others may choose to reread a book to find evidence that disproves a hunch recorded on the class chart.

During the share, the two partnerships at each basket will engage in cross-partnership talk, whereby the partnerships will talk about the big ideas they have discovered about the texts. (This is a wonderful opportunity for students to work in small groups, learn from one another, and deepen their understanding of the work being studied. Students can use their prerecorded reading center activity sheet when sharing their ideas.)

What hunches are we gathering about our characters?

Maisy:

Biscuit:

Piggy:

Monkey:

Frog and Toad

Partners record their hunches on sticky notes and place them on a class chart. I use the chart in subsequent mini-lessons to share different hunches partnerships are formulating about the same character and across characters.

Keeping Students Motivated

Before this session, I like to add one or two new books to each book basket. This is helpful in keeping students motivated and excited to work in their reading centers.

Day 6: How did it go?

I introduce and review the center packet activity sheet titled, "Thinking About Our _____ Reading Centers," which asks students to reflect on the reading center study. (An evaluation form given at the end of a nonfiction study appears at right and a reproducible form for an ABC study is included on page 107.) I find this activity to be very informative because it encourages students to reflect on their partnership performance, learning, and possible interest in a back-to-back cycle of the study.

Students complete the reading center evaluation sheet. Partners can help one another read the questions listed on the sheet.

In the remaining time, partners read one last book from their reading center basket and discuss all the ideas the class and their partnership have identified about the topic or genre they have read.

How Can Teachers Help Partners Focus Their Book Conversation and Provide Instruction During Conferences?

While partnerships are reading and talking about their reading center books, I confer with them to listen to their ideas and to help them guide, focus, and extend their thinking. I usually confer with four partnerships over the course of each reading center session. (In this way I am able to confer with each partnership at least twice during the six- to-seven-day study.) I use many of the phrases and questions listed below to help partnerships deepen and enhance their conversations about their books. I also use my conferring experiences to select partners who can help model book-talk strategies with the class during our share time.

The following three strategies focus my teaching and guide students' talk during a conference. Included are suggestions for how to phrase questions to support students' learning.

Name: Alessandra   **Date:** 3/4/0 ?

Thinking About Our Nonfiction Reading Centers

1. Who was your reading center partner?

   Claire

2. How did you and your partner work together?

   😊   😐   ☹️

3. What nonfiction center would you like to be in for our next cycle?

   Vallcinos

4. What was the most interesting thing you learned?

   How much Bears can way.

At the end of a reading center study, students reflect and evaluate their partnership work.

Partnership Self-Evaluation Activity Sheets

Partners benefit from reflecting on their experience working together. When they have completed their evaluations, I ask partners to share their reflections and discuss how they can improve their partner work for the next reading center cycle.

1. **Encourage partners to show the places in the books that support their hunch.**
   - ◆ "Can you show me where?" or "Can you show me the part in the book that makes you think that?"
   - ◆ "This is a big idea you are having. You should use stick on-notes to record the places in the book where you are noticing this happening."
   - ◆ "I don't know what you mean. Can you show me the pictures or sentences where you noticed that in the book?"

2. **Name what partners are doing to help their work become more purposeful.**
   - ◆ "So, you two are gathering information on butterflies . . . ."
   - ◆ "You and your partner are comparing how the character's behavior is the same in each book."

3. **Scaffold great partner talks by teaching conversation techniques including adding on to what your partner has said, agreeing/ disagreeing with your partner's ideas, asking your partner's opinion, and so on. (Chapter 4 provides ways to teach these talk habits to students.)**
   - ◆ "Ask your partner what he/she thinks about your hunch that Biscuit is an adventurous puppy."
   - ◆ "Do you agree with your partner that Toad is a good friend to Frog? Why or why not? You could say something like, 'I disagree/agree with you because . . .'"

From *Growing Readers: Units of Study in the Primary Classroom* by Kathy Collins. © 2004, with permission of Stenhouse Publishers.

Assessing the Book Talk of Reading Center Partnerships

During my conferring, I assess how my students are talking, provide explicit instruction to meet the individual needs of each partnership, and use this information to plan for follow-up mini-lessons. If I notice, for instance, that students are not looking for evidence in their texts when developing hunches, I plan for mini-lessons that will teach this technique. In other words, my conferring notes help me provide in-the-moment instruction as well as plan purposeful mini-lessons. (Chapter 7 provides a variety of ways teachers can assess partnerships and plan for instruction.) I also use my ongoing assessment to keep a record of phrases partners are using to keep their talk going. I accumulate this data during my conferences and then review them repeatedly during our mini-lessons and shares. The table on the next page outlines strategies partners use to focus book talk and related phrases they can use that signal each strategy.

◆ STRATEGIES FOR ASSESSING BOOK TALK ◆	
Book-Talk Strategy	**Signal Phrases Partners Can Use**
Identify overlapping information and/or discrepancies between books.	*"This book is/isn't like the other books in our basket because . . . ."* (Partners use this phrase when they notice how a book does/doesn't provide evidence for their hunch.)
Accumulate information about a topic from a variety of texts.	*"So far I've learned that . . . ."* (Partners use this phrase when they are reading texts, making comparisons between texts, and developing hunches about their texts.)
Pay attention to surprising information, new information, information that contradicts prior knowledge and beliefs.	*"I didn't know that . . . ."* *"I used to think that . . . ."* *"That doesn't seem right to me because . . ."* (Partners use these phrases when they are modifying and/or disproving a hunch.)
Pay attention to new wonderings.	*"I wonder why . . . ."* (Partners use this phrase often at the beginning of a study as they begin to explore the new texts.)
Attend to characteristics of the book, genre, or author.	*"I notice that . . . ."* (Partners use this phrase when comparing the texts in their baskets.)
Plan for reading and book-talk work.	*"Tomorrow we should look for all the places where . . . ."* (Partners use this phrase when they are gathering hunches and plan to keep this line of thinking in mind when they read the next text.)
Look for evidence.	*"We are looking for all the places where . . . ."* (Partners use this phrase when looking at the print and illustrations that provide support for their hunch.)
Discuss/disagree.	*"We are talking about . . . ."* *"My partner thinks . . . but I think . . . ."* (Partners use these phrases when they are debating whether a proposed hunch is true and finding the necessary evidence to prove or disprove the hunch.)

Adapted from "Thinking to Notice and Support in Reading Centers" in *Growing Readers: Units of Study in the Primary Classroom* by Kathy Collins. © 2004, with permission of Stenhouse Publishers.

Back-to-Back Studies of Reading Centers

As part of the assessment process, I also consider whether a second study of the reading center, or "back-to-back cycles," would support the needs and interest of my students. During a character study, for example, students are often eager for the opportunity to read a second character series based on the enthusiastic response of another partnership that read about the character during the first cycle.

If I decide to have the class engage in back-to-back cycles, I use a format similar to the first study and begin the second study right after the first one. (Because the baskets of books remain the same, this can easily be accomplished.) I have found that students are typically capable of delving deeper during a second study because of their experiences during the first one—and this makes back-to-back studies an incredibly valuable and worthwhile experience for students.

◆

Through their work as partners in reading centers, students are able to build on their partner work while broadening their talk practices in a new format. By reading and talking about specific kinds of texts, partners are able to study and learn key concepts of science and social studies and fundamental reading and writing conventions of specific genres. In addition, using a balance of daily partnership reading and reading centers in a primary classroom helps to motivate students with meaningful and purposeful reading and talking practices. Both types of partnership work enrich students' reading lives with exposure to a wide variety of literature.

The next chapter outlines a detailed ABC reading center study that can meet the needs of first, second, and third graders. The ABC study can be implemented to teach a wide range of reading skills to students, such as concepts about print, word attack strategies, comprehension, inferences, and drawing conclusions. Through their partnership reading and talking, students practice these key skills using exceptional picture books.

Chapter 6

Reading Partnerships in Action:
An In-Depth Reading Center Study

This chapter takes a close look at an ABC reading center study that can be successfully implemented with reading partnerships in any primary classroom. Chapter 5 provides the background; it outlines how reading centers can support students' work in reading partnerships and provides organization, management, and instruction tips for integrating reading centers with your ongoing partner reading work.

When you choose a topic for a reading center study, consider the curriculum as well as the needs, interests, and abilities of your students. For example, during my class's science study of weather, I organize nonfiction weather reading centers through which students learn concepts about weather as well as strategies for reading nonfiction texts. Using subject-based reading centers allows you to integrate curriculum areas, thereby increasing student learning and managing your teaching time effectively.

By planning and organizing reading centers in advance, you can formulate what you want students to learn from their reading center work. When I plan my curriculum pacing calendar for the year, for example, I decide what reading center studies will support the curriculum. Furthermore, by outlining the specific purposes of each study in advance, I am able to gather appropriate books for the center study.

◆ SAMPLE READING CENTER PACING CALENDAR ◆			
Topic	**Time of Year**	**Purpose**	**How It Supports Reading Partnerships**
ABC Study	October	Students learn to look at texts (words and pictures) closely.	Partners learn to stay longer and talk more about texts.
Character Study	December	Students learn about the story elements of fiction (e.g., character, plot, setting, change, movement through time).	Partners make connections between texts and develop hunches and big ideas about their thinking.
Friendship	January	Students learn social skills and conflict resolution strategies.	Partners make text-to-self and text-to-text connections.
Author	February	Students study the writing techniques (e.g., craft) of an author in depth.	Partners identify craft techniques of an author's work and compare/ contrast his or her style with that of other authors.
Nonfiction	March/April	Students learn reading strategies specific to the nonfiction genre (e.g., naming subjects, reading captions, using the table of contents).	Partners read, talk, and learn from texts written at a variety of reading levels and written with different formats (e.g., question/answer).
Poetry	May	Students learn poetry techniques (e.g., imagery, figurative language, line repetition).	Partners practice oral reading skills while reading poems aloud, using tone, rhythm, and so on.

◆ An ABC Reading Center Partnership Study ◆

An ABC study is an exciting study for students of all primary ages. Through my exploration of ABC books, I have discovered that the majority of alphabet texts serve a wide range of reading abilities. ABC books are often characterized, for example, by lengthy text, complex vocabulary, and higher-level concepts. Even more surprising is that frequently the texts that are wordless or limited in print inspire the most in-depth book talk. Most ABC books, in fact, support fluent as well as emergent readers and nonreaders. (I have included a suggested bibliography of alphabet books on page 90.)

◆ WHAT ARE THE PURPOSES OF ABC READING CENTERS? ◆

ABC reading centers are a great way to introduce students to reading centers. Because students often have prior experience with alphabet books, they are ready to participate in ABC reading centers with great confidence and enthusiasm in the early fall. The centers provide a great way to reinforce general reading skills and beginning reading partnership practices.

◆ WHY USE ABC READING CENTERS? ◆	
Benefits to the Reading Curriculum	**Benefits to Reading Partnerships**
ABC reading centers: ◆ provide practice for reading readiness skills (e.g., letter-sound correspondence, picture-word connection). ◆ support early reading strategies (e.g., looking at the pictures, looking at the beginning letter of words). ◆ offer students opportunities to practice choosing books at the appropriate reading levels. ◆ encourage students to explore the classroom library.	ABC reading centers: ◆ motivate partners to compare and contrast texts read. ◆ provide support for book conversations around familiar topics and text structure. ◆ encourage partners to stay longer with texts. ◆ provide opportunities for students to work with different partners.

SUGGESTED ABC BIBLIOGRAPHY

ABC by Bruno Munari

ABC by Dr. Seuss

ABCs: The American Indian Way by R. Red Hawk

A Is for Artist by the Getty Museum

A, My Name Is Alice by J. Bayer

A to Z Look and See by Audean Johnson

A You're Adorable by Martha Alexander

Alison's Zinnia by Anita Lobel

All Aboard ABC by Doug Magee and Robert Newman

Alligators All Around by Maurice Sendak

Alphabatics by Suse Macdonald

Alphabears by Kathleen Hague

Alphabet City by Stephen T. Johnson

Animalia by Graeme Base

Anno's Alphabet by Mitsumasa Anno

Ape in a Cape: An Alphabet of Odd Animals by Fritz Eichenberg

Arlene Alda's ABC by Arlene Alda

Ashanti to Zulu: African Traditions by Margaret Musgrove

Brian Wildsmith's ABC by Brian Wildsmith

Bugs and Beasties by Cheryl Nathan

Caribbean Alphabet by Frané Lessac

Chicka Chicka Boom Boom by Bill Martin

City Seen From A to Z by Rachel Isadora

David McPhail's Animals A to Z by David McPhail

Easy as Pie by Marcia and Michael Folsom

Eating the Alphabet by Lois Ehlert

Eating the Alphabet: Fruits and Vegetables From A–Z by Lois Short

From Acorn to Zoo by Satoshi Kitamura

Gretchen's ABC by G. D. Simpson

Handsigns: A Sign Language Alphabet by Kathleen Fain

Harold's ABC by Crockett Johnson

Hosies's Alphabet by Leonard Baskin

I Spy a Freight Train by Lucy Micklethwait

It Begins With an A by Stephanie Calmenson

John Burningham's ABC by John Burningham

K is for Kissing a Cool Kangaroo by Giles Andreae

Many Nations: An Alphabet of Native America by Joseph Bruchac

On Market Street by Arnold and Anita Lobel

Project ABC by Idalia Rosario

Q Is for Duck by Mary Elting and Michael Folsom

The ABC Bunny by Wanda Gág

The ABC Mystery by Doug Cushman

The Accidental Zucchini by Max Grover

The Alphabet Book by P. D. Eastman

The Alphabet Tree by Leo Lionni

The Calypso Alphabet by J. Agard

The Desert Alphabet Book by Jerry Pallota

The Dinosaur Alphabet Book by Jerry Pallota

The Dominie Alphabet Book by T. Greven

The Flower Alphabet Book by Jerry Pallota

The Furry Animal Alphabet Book by Jerry Pallota

The Handmade Alphabet Book by Laura Rankin

The Icky Bug Alphabet Book by Jerry Pallota

The Ocean Alphabet Book by Jerry Pallota

The Underwater Alphabet Book by Jerry Pallota

The Yucky Reptile Book by Jerry Pallota

The Z Was Zapped by Chris Van Allsburg

Big Books

Farm Alphabet Book by Jane Miller

Here Comes Hungry Albert by Pat Whitehead

Let's Go to the Zoo by Pat Whitehead

Getting Students Ready for ABC Reading Centers

To prepare my class for our first reading center study, I do several things. In September, I immerse students in ABC books through our daily read alouds. By sharing ABC books with students and explaining that they will be reading many similar books during our upcoming ABC reading centers, I create an air of excitement about reading ABC books.

I carefully select a range of ABC books to read aloud. For example, I read some that give information about a subject (e.g., kinds of ocean life), some that have "tricks" (e.g., hidden pictures, riddles), some that are wordless and rely solely on pictures for meaning, and some that are written in a question-and-answer format. By reading aloud a variety of texts to my students, they are able to see that the different formats require that we read the books in different ways. I also encourage students to bring in ABC books from home to add to our class collection. The opportunity for students to help create the baskets of books for the study builds a sense of community in the classroom.

Finally and most important, I prepare my class for reading centers by introducing daily reading partnerships early in September. As described in Chapters 3 and 4, I teach students specific routines, expectations, and book talk strategies to use in both daily reading partnerships and reading center partnerships.

An ABC Reading Center Study, Day by Day

♦ THE MINI-LESSONS ♦

I usually spend eight to ten days on our ABC study over the course of a few weeks. I schedule reading centers every other day, during our partner reading time. The following is a suggested outline and sequence of mini-lessons that can be easily modified and adapted for students of varying ages and abilities.

Day 1: What ABC books are in each basket?

Once I have collected an assortment of ABC books, I group the books into six baskets. In each basket, I place six to eight ABC books that vary in style, format, and text difficulty. My decision to include texts of all reading levels in each basket is based on my desire to have partnerships that are not ability based. The number of baskets I create depends on the number of students in my classroom. I usually have two partnerships share a basket.

To begin the center study, I explain to students that they will spend two days previewing each basket. I call these two days our "exploring days." By allowing time for students to preview each basket, they are able to choose a basket they are interested in for the study.

During my first mini-lesson I demonstrate how to preview books. (The term *preview* is familiar to my students because we use it whenever we begin a new text in our daily read-aloud and guided-reading sessions.) I teach students to preview books by looking at the cover illustration, reading the book title, taking a picture walk, and reading the first page of the text.

I record their reading responsibilities on our lesson focus chart.

Day 1:
Explore and preview the books in three center baskets.

On exploration days, I have students work with their daily reading partner. I assign two partnerships to each center basket. (I use different-colored baskets so that students can differentiate between them.) Partners spend about seven minutes exploring and previewing the books in each basket. Every seven minutes, I signal for students to move to another basket. Before students move to a new basket, I always ask them to consider whether they liked the books in the basket they were exploring. I encourage them to list in their reading journal the baskets they are most interested in working with during the study, so that they can make an informed decision when they sign up for a center.

Day 2: What ABC basket will you choose?
The mini-lesson of the second day mirrors the first day, during which students review how to explore and preview texts. I explain that at the end of the exploration session, each student will choose a basket to work with during the study.

I record their reading responsibilities on our lesson focus chart.

Day 2:
Explore and preview the books in three more baskets. Choose an ABC center basket. Decide on partnerships for your basket. Begin to sketch your ABC center study packet cover.

Matching Students to Center Baskets

When I am selecting volunteers for each basket, I focus on choosing groups of students who will work well together, keeping in mind their personalities, behaviors, and abilities. My goal is to create an academically and socially balanced group of students at each center.

After students have explored the remaining baskets, I gather the class on the carpet and display a chart where I have listed the six center baskets by color. As I name each center, students volunteer to work with each basket. (At the start of the year we spend a lot of time discussing that throughout the year when we are making choices for our literacy, math, and reading centers, we may not always get our first choice and should therefore have several choices in mind.)

As I select students, they sign their names on a poster titled "What ABC Reading Center Did You Choose?" After all students are assigned to a center, I have the groups meet and divide into two partnerships. Then I hand out the ABC center study packet to each partnership. (A reproducible of the center packet is included at the end of the chapter.)

Partners spend the remaining time sketching and coloring the cover of their center study packets, which are kept in the center baskets along with the books. Each packet contains the activity sheets the students will complete as part of the study. (The mini-lessons for days 4, 5, 6, 7, and 9 describe how students complete the activity sheets.)

What ABC Reading Center Did You Choose?

red
1. Alex Q
2. Jason
3. Tiffany
4. Callie

orange
1. Michael
2. Brian
3. Solange
4.

blue
1. Landon
2. Molly
3. Dennis
4. Brittany

green
1. Lily .M
2. Taina
3. Andy
4. Lily W.

purple
1. Aidan
2. Alessandra
3. Rebecca

4. Jordan

Students spend two days exploring each center, getting familiar with all the books. Then they choose the one that interests them most. (I organize baskets by color.)

Cover of ABC center packet, page 104. After they have chosen the ABC book basket they are interested in reading, students illustrate the cover of their ABC reading center packets.

My Alphabet Reading Center Study

Name: Brittany

My Alphabet Reading Center Study

Name: Lily. M

Day 3: Which book will you read and how will you read it?

I begin the mini-lesson by explaining to students that each day they work in their reading centers, they will be reading one new book. (The goal is for partners to do focused work around one book each day rather than to read several books quickly.)

Giving Partners Choices in Ways They Can Read Together

I find that partners develop ways to read their books besides the choral, echo and taking-turns format. (I intentionally leave the assignment of how to read and talk about books open-ended and I am always amazed at the creative and unusual ways partners interact with the texts.) When I confer with partners on that first day, I focus on how partners are choosing a text and reading it. The observations I make during my conferences help me plan my upcoming mini-lessons as well as identify partners who can model successful reading practices as part of our share.

I choose a volunteer to act as my reading partner. First, we decide how we will select a book each day. (Often partners take turns choosing books, as described in Chapter 3.) Next, we preview the book and decide how we will read it. (Partners may use the text format to make this decision. For example, a text written in question-and-answer format works well with partners taking turns while reading. Chapter 3 describes several ways partners can read texts together.)

During my mini-lesson role play of how partners can read an ABC book, I engage my partner in a conversation about the book by asking, "How is this ABC book special or unique? How is it different from or the same as other ABC books we have read? How is it different from or the same as books that are not ABC books?"

I record their reading responsibilities on our lesson focus chart.

Day 3: ————————————————————————————————
Choose one book to read. Decide how you will read it. Read it. Talk about the book. What do you notice? What is unique about your book? How is it the same or different from other books?
————————————————————————————————

At the end of our partner reading session, I share with the class that I observed some very interesting ways partners were reading their texts. I select several partnerships to demonstrate their unique reading practices.

One partnership, for example, when reading *Anno's Alphabet*, went beyond naming the object illustrated for each alphabet letter. They discovered that the shape of each letter could be found as part of each object illustrated. Because this book was not in every center basket, I asked the class if other partnerships could find this technique in other texts they were reading. In another instance, the partnerships that were reading the books *What Is It?* and *I Spy* each shared how they read their books by having one partner read the clues and the other partner guess the answer. We discussed whether other ABC books could be read using this technique.

Day 4: What are you noticing?

For the mini-lesson, I begin by reminding students that they will choose a

second book to read with their partner. We quickly review some of the ways partners may choose to read the books based on the previous center share.

I explain to the class that today they will begin to compare two books they have read. I ask them to consider, "How are your books similar?" and "What are you noticing about your ABC books?" (I purposely leave these questions open-ended so that partners have the freedom to explore their texts in their own way.)

I record their reading responsibilities on our lesson focus chart.

Day 4:

Choose a second book to read. Decide how you will read it. Read it. Talk about the book. Think about the two books you've read. What are you noticing about ABC books? Record on page 1 of your center packet the titles of the ABC books you have read with your partner.

At the end of our partner reading session, I choose several partnerships to share what they noticed about the two books they have read. (It is helpful for the class if the partners display the text pages to the class as the partners share their findings.)

In past ABC reading center studies, partners have noticed a variety of important characteristics, including that both of their books had photographs, that the alphabet letters on each page were written at the top and with capital letters, and that both of their books included all the letters of the alphabet in the same order, A–Z. These findings helped students develop hunches and big ideas about their books, which led to their understanding of the text structure of ABC books during the study.

Day 5: What hunches are you gathering?
To begin the mini-lesson, I ask reading partners to turn and talk with one another about what they noticed in the previous center session about ABC books. I explain to students that while they are reading their third book, they should keep in mind what they've found out about ABC books. I share that we can call these "hunches." I define hunches as ideas partners develop when reading and talking about related books. I explain that as partners read more books, they may change their original

---

Name Sandra   Date 10/ 12 |02

ABC Center Study

1. What ABC center did you choose?

   blue

2. What ABC books are you and your partner reading?

   A to Z Look and See

   The Alphabet Book

   Eating the Alphabet

3. What are you noticing about ABC books?

   ABC book hav wrds that strts

   with the ladr on the paj. You find

   theing.

First page of ABC center packet, page 105. Students show what they are learning about ABC book structure.

hunch (revise their thinking) or disprove their hunch based on new evidence found in other books. I emphasize how readers support hunches across texts using text words and illustrations.

To help partners compare texts, I demonstrate with three familiar ABC read-aloud books. I show students that by laying the three books out side by side, I can reread, compare, and locate evidence to support my hunch in all three.

I encourage students to record their hunches on sticky notes and place them on our class chart titled "What Hunches Do We Have About ABC Books?" (sticky notes should be kept in the center baskets for easy student access.)

I record their reading responsibilities on our lesson focus chart.

Day 5: ————————————————————————————————————

Choose a third book to read. While you are reading the third book, keep in mind your hunch about ABC books. Compare your three books. Does your hunch still work? Did you gather any new hunches about ABC books? Write your hunches on sticky notes and put them on the class chart. Record on page 1 of your center packet the ABC books you are reading with your partner.

At the end of the reading session, partners share their recorded hunches. Some examples of hunches my students have developed are ABC books go in alphabetical order, ABC books have letters in them, ABC books have pictures, ABC books have pictures that match letters of the alphabet, ABC books always start with the letter a, ABC books help you learn letters and sounds, ABC books can be fiction or nonfiction.

Day 6: What hunches can be proved?
For the mini-lesson, I review the hunches partners have gathered and recorded on the class chart "What Hunches Do We Have About ABC Books?" I encourage several partnerships to share with the class their books, hunches, and the evidence in each text that supports their hunches.

I explain to students that sometimes a hunch we have may need to be changed as we read new books. Partners can change their hunch by making word changes. For example, instead of saying "all ABC books . . ." partners could say "many, some, or often ABC books . . ." Or sometimes rather than changing a hunch, a partnership may choose to disprove a hunch as they read more. To include the revisions partners make to their initial hunches, I add the question "Did any of our hunches get disproved?" to the bottom

half of our hunches chart. I encourage partners as they read and talk to make necessary changes such as the wording of their hunch on a sticky note (e.g., from "all" to "many/some") or to move the sticky note to the bottom of the class chart if they are disproving the hunch. (Having partners make changes and/or disprove hunches pushes them to think deeply and talk specifically about texts they are reading.)

I record their reading responsibilities on our lesson focus chart.

Day 6:

Choose a fourth book to read. Read the text, keeping in mind your hunches. Discuss with your partner whether your hunch is still true. If not, can you modify your hunch by changing some words? If you disprove your hunch, move your sticky note to the bottom of the chart and be ready to explain why it has been disproved. Record on page 1 of your center packet the ABC books you are reading with your partner.

At the end of the reading session, partners who have changed a hunch share their findings. In a previous study, for example, one partnership whose hunch was that there was a zebra on every "z" page, modified their hunch from "All ABC books have a zebra on the 'z' page" to "Many ABC books have a zebra on the 'z' page." Another partnership whose hunch was "All ABC books are search-and-find books" changed their hunch to "Some ABC books are search-and-find books."

A few partnerships that chose to disprove rather than change their hunches also share their work. For example, a partnership whose hunch was "All ABC books have the alphabet letter at the top of the page" moved their sticky note to the disproved section of the class chart after reading a text that had the letter of each page in the bottom left-hand corner of each page.

I have found that the challenge of finding evidence to disprove hunches is very motivating and exciting for students. When partners present a hunch and others have evidence to support or disprove it, a lively discussion takes place in the classroom. (I teach students that when debating or disagreeing with others, they can say "I disagree because . . ." to ensure that their ideas are conveyed in a manner that does not criticize or judge the ideas of others negatively.)

Partners record on sticky notes hunches they are gathering about ABC books. If they find examples that disprove their initial hunch, they move the sticky note to the bottom of the chart to show it has been disproved.

Name Lily, M   Date Oct. 22

What Are You Noticing?

Write some new things you are noticing about ABC books.

1. Some hav pekchrs.

2. Some hav wrds.

3. All abc boks go in ordr

Second page of ABC center packet, page 106. Students record their hunches.

Day 7: What hunches have we disproved?

By this time in the study, students feel like experts about their basket of books. To keep the enthusiasm alive, I usually add one or two new books to each basket.

We begin the mini-lesson by reviewing the sticky notes placed on the hunches chart. One partnership shares how they disproved a hunch using evidence on specific text pages.

As part of the day's partnership work, students are asked to read a new book, gather further evidence to support or disprove their hunches, discover new hunches, and record their hunches again on page 2 of their center packet. I explain that hunches that have been proven over many books can be also be called "big ideas."

I record their reading responsibilities on our lesson focus chart.

Day 7:

Reread a favorite book or read a new one from your basket. On page 2 of your ABC packet, record the hunches you have developed and have proved. Share your hunches with the other partnership at your basket.

TIPS FOR USING ACTIVITY SHEETS IN CENTER STUDIES

◆ Even young students can effectively use a variety of graphic organizers during their reading center studies. (You'll want to offer those graphic organizers that are most helpful to your students and supportive of the study's purpose. For example, in a character study you might have students complete a Venn diagram when comparing two characters.)

◆ Make sure the majority of time students spend in their centers is on reading and talking about their texts. Schedule other time during the day for students to complete their written work.

◆ Be selective and limit the number of activity sheets students are using for centers. In fact, if you feel that students have become too dependent on teacher-provided graphic organizers, you might have students record their thinking on sticky notes.

Day 8: What will you share with another partnership?

Assigning two partnerships to a center allows partners to "cross-talk" or share ideas with one another. When partnerships share with one another what they have learned, students accumulate more knowledge. In order for two partnerships to engage in a purposeful, focused conversation, I have the partnerships that share a basket meet at the beginning of the session to decide what they will talk about. Next, each partnership spends time reading, keeping in mind the talk focus they've agreed upon. Then, the two partnerships reconvene and engage in their cross-talk conversation using their books to support their thinking.

To demonstrate cross-talk between partnerships, I choose two partnerships to model this strategy using some of our class ABC read alouds. (I choose these two partnerships in advance so they can meet to decide what they want to talk about and can prepare by reading and talking about the material.)

I begin the mini-lesson by explaining that the two partnerships that share a basket of ABC books will be meeting to talk about their center work. I outline the process as follows: (1) partnerships meet and choose a conversation topic, (2) partnerships read texts and prepare for the talk, and (3) partnerships meet again and engage in a conversation.

The class brainstorms examples of ways partnerships can focus their conversation, which I record on a chart titled "What Can Partnerships Talk About?" In a previous study, for example, the chart included the questions, What was our favorite ABC book and why? How were our ABC books similar/different? What format did the author and illustrator use when writing and illustrating the books? What hunches did we gather about ABC books?

The volunteer partnerships model their cross-talk conversation beginning by sharing the topic they have planned for their talk. During a previous study, for example, the volunteer partnerships decided to focus their conversation around unique techniques illustrators use in the pictures to help the reader learn more about the alphabet. They chose to work with a text that they each had a copy of *K Is for Kissing a Cool Kangaroo* by Giles Andreae. One partnership observed that on each letter page the rhyme included a few words with the corresponding letter ("B is for busy and big bumblebee."), all of which were illustrated. Furthermore, when they looked carefully at each illustration, they also noticed that there were other pictures beginning with the letter that were not mentioned in the rhyme (for example, on the "b" page there also was a bowl and ball in the illustration). The second partnership

---

Encouraging Partner Cross-talk

Remind students that partnerships must engage in a conversation, not a share. Each partnership's responsibility is to listen to the other partnership and add on, respond, and react to what is being said. (Chapter 4 describes how to teach students conversation strategies.)

added on to this idea by observing how in each of the book's illustrations there was at least one animal not mentioned in the rhyme that began with the corresponding letter (for example, on the "b" page, there were a bear, a beaver, and a bull). The partnerships eagerly went through the text, page by page, and had an interactive game of finding the "hidden animal" on each page. They noticed the only page to break the pattern was the "z" page ("And Z is for zebra—now how did you guess?!") and decided that the illustrator was probably unable to think of another animal besides zebra that begins with the letter z.

The conversation between the two partnerships continued with them focusing on how the author and illustrator sometimes connected the text and illustrations of two consecutive pages (i.e., two consecutive letters). One example they discussed was the rhyme that connected the "m" and "n" pages, "M is for mischievous monkey and mat" and "N is for naughty. No, don't do that!" They noticed that the rhyme over the two pages was a short story of the monkeys' behavior of acting naughty and getting scolded by their parents. As the partnerships went through the book, they identified and discussed several other examples in which two consecutive letter pages created a rhyme that was a mini-story.

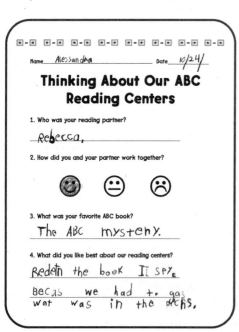

Third page of ABC center packet, page 107. Students assess their partnership experience.

During the role-playing of cross-talk conversations, I coach partnerships to listen to one another so that they can add on and connect new thoughts to the previous one shared. In this way we demonstrate how partnerships engage in conversations rather than shares.

I record their reading responsibilities on our lesson focus chart.

Day 8:
Meet with the other partnership at your center. Decide what you will talk about. What text or texts will you use? Prepare for your conversation by reading a new text or rereading familiar texts with your talk focus in mind. Have a conversation with the other partnership.

Day 9: Thinking about your ABC reading center
For the mini-lesson, I review the evaluation sheet in the center packet. Students, for example, consider questions such as, How did you and your partner work together? What was your favorite ABC book? What did you like best about our reading centers? (Chapters 5 and 7 describe in detail a variety of ways to assess reading partnerships.)

I record their reading responsibilities on our lesson focus chart.

Day 9:
Complete page 3 of your center packet. Think about how your partnership went during our study. Reread a favorite ABC book from your basket with your partner. Discuss why it's a favorite.

At the end of the reading session, students gather with their completed evaluation forms and share what they liked best about their center experience. I may ask the class to discuss whether they have interest in doing a second cycle or back-to-back cycles of ABC books. I display completed student packets and the class hunches chart around the classroom. This chart serves as a classroom resource. For example, when we read and discuss a book during read aloud, I often use the hunches recorded on the chart to highlight how readers "grow" ideas about the books they've read.

Day 10 (optional): What information will you hold on to?
Based on students' interest in our study, I decide whether I will extend our study and have my students participate in additional activities to share what they have learned. I call these "teaching times." (I find these activities to be extremely valuable and enjoyable for students, especially when our study is intense or we do back-to-back cycles.)

One activity is to have partnerships of different center baskets meet and share some of the things they have learned. Students like this opportunity because they are able to spend time working with books in other baskets. Partnerships also feel empowered by the chance to teach another partnership about what they have learned from their basket of books.

To demonstrate, I spend a few minutes at the start of the mini-lesson commenting that over the period of our study the class has learned a great deal of information about ABC books. I explain that it's impossible to remember all the information we've read, so it's important to consider what we value most about what we've learned. To help students, I ask, "What are the most important, impressive, exciting things you've learned about ABC books that you would like to remember and share with others?" Once partners are focused on one or two important ideas, they can choose another partnership to meet and share with. It is helpful to point out to students that the partnership that is listening should ask questions of the "teaching partnership" to help make the share a meaningful experience.

A second way I provide my students with a teaching time is to have them work on an end-of-study project, which serves as a permanent

At the end of our study one year, students chose to make an ABC big book as a class project. Students each worked on one letter page. We modeled our page layout (letter, word, and picture placement) on Rachel Isadora's *City Seen From A to Z*.

record of the information they want to hold on to after the study ends. Projects are open-ended activities that allow students to demonstrate their expertise on a given subject. Each partnership decides what information they want to share and how to present it. Projects are valuable because they encourage partnerships to reread books and reflect on what they've learned. Projects also allow for what students have learned to be differentiated; partners are able to engage in projects that best reflect and support their developmental abilities.

During one ABC study, each partnership created their own ABC book following the format and style of one book they had read. One partnership used *All Aboard ABC* by Doug Nagee and Robert Newman as a model. This book features a train-related word for each letter of the alphabet. At the time, our class was also studying the local park as part of our social studies curriculum, so the partnership made an alphabet book featuring park-related words. For instance, for the letter *z*, they drew and labeled a picture of the zookeeper we had interviewed. (See the box below for more project suggestions.)

End-of-Center-Study Project	Example
ABC books	Make an ABC book using one of the formats studied such as question-and-answer, search-and-find, or theme.
top ten lists	Write a top ten hunches list or top ten favorite texts.
Venn diagram posters	Create a giant Venn diagram comparing and contrasting features of two ABC books.
graphs	Make a bar graph that shows which ABC texts classmates like best.
advertisements	Write a must-read! ad for a popular ABC book.
three-dimensional letter figures	Draw a large letter on to two sheets of paper. Cut the letters out and place them back to back. Fasten them around the edges, leaving an opening wide enough to stuff, and then stuff the letter shape with newspaper. Close up the opening and hang from a string.

Since my students enjoy making elaborate projects, I have them complete their work during choice time rather than during reading workshop. Upon completion, I have each partnership share their project with the class as well as display the projects in our classroom.

◆

The work of daily reading partnerships—specifically reading and talking strategies—can be strengthened by students' participation in reading center studies throughout the year. The detailed outline I've provided of my ABC reading center study shows how reading center studies (1) allow students to work and grow as readers with different reading partners, (2) develop their book-talk skills by offering them texts to compare and contrast in a focused conversation, (3) integrate concepts being studied in other curriculum areas, (4) provide opportunities to explore different genres, and (5) create a fresh forum to review or introduce more sophisticated reading partnership skills. Chapter 7 describes how to assess student work in partnerships.

My Alphabet
Reading Center Study

Name:_____

Name_____ Date_____

ABC Center Study

1. What ABC center did you choose?

_____

2. What ABC books are you and your partner reading?

_____

_____

_____

3. What are you noticing about ABC books?

_____

_____

_____

Name_____ Date_____

What Are You Noticing?

Write some new things you are noticing about ABC books.

1. _____

2. _____

3. _____

Partner Reading: A Way to Help All Readers Grow • Scholastic Teaching Resources

Name_____ Date_____

Thinking About Our ABC Reading Centers

1. Who was your reading partner?

_____

2. How did you and your partner work together?

3. What was your favorite ABC book?

_____

4. What did you like best about our reading centers?

_____

_____

Partner Reading: A Way to Help All Readers Grow • Scholastic Teaching Resources

Chapter 7

Assessing Reading Partnerships

Assessment, an essential component of the teaching and learning process, greatly impacts the growth of early readers. This chapter specifically explores how you can make assessment of reading partnerships productive and meaningful for both you and your students—without its being a laborious process. In fact, the assessment strategies described below can be done with simple tools that you use on an ongoing basis.

Why Assess Reading Partnerships and Not Just Reading Skills?

You'll want to assess reading partnerships in order to determine both the academic and social needs of your students. You can use these observations to evaluate and consider partnership longevity, efficiency, and productivity—as well as to show evidence of growth toward meeting grade-level reading objectives.

What to Assess in Reading Partnerships

Reading Level Assessments

See Chapter 2 for a discussion of formal and informal assessment methods you can use to both determine the reading abilities of your students and pair up students as reading partners.

Partnerships should be assessed on their reading, talking, and behavioral abilities. Specifically, this includes students' abilities to comprehend texts and to read and respond effectively in a discussion with a partner. During a fall unit of study, for instance, when reading partnerships are first introduced, you may assess partners on their abilities to share books, support one another with reading strategies, and engage in beginning book talk. (As described in Chapter 3, the routines and guidelines of partnerships must be firmly established before partners can be expected to engage in deeper book talk.) Throughout the year, as you introduce more sophisticated strategies, you can modify your expectations of the partner work to reflect more in-depth reading and talking skills. (Chapters 3, 4, 5, and 6 include suggested mini-lessons for teaching students book-talk strategies.)

Because every teacher designs and implements his or her own units of study for teaching partnership skills and strategies, what teachers decide to assess their students on will vary. Some teachers, for example, may spend a lot of time teaching their students ways to extend their book talk and consequently focus their assessment on those talk strategies. Other teachers, however, may focus their teaching and assessment on specific skills taught as part of a reading center study. Page 124 offers a reproducible checklist of suggested skills and strategies to assess. You may prefer to develop your own checklist using the reproducible on page 125.

TIPS FOR ASSESSING READING PARTNERSHIPS

◆ When planning a unit of study focusing on reading partnerships, identify the skills students are expected to master and use these skills as guidelines for your assessment.

◆ When assessing reading partnerships, evaluate students on the talk they are engaged in with one another (the content of their conversations and their ability to communicate with a partner), rather than on their reading abilities. The quality of their talk will show their level of comprehension. Some students, for example, may have a limited or literal understanding while others are able to infer and develop ideas and hunches.

◆ When assessing reading partnerships, consider student age, grade level, partnership experience, and knowledge of the material being read.

Listed below are key objectives and focus questions you can use when assessing your reading partnerships. (Sample reproducibles for recording assessment of student performance are included at the end of the chapter.)

◆ ASSESSING PARTNERSHIPS ◆	
Key Objectives for Partnerships	**Specific Focus Questions**
Partners talk, using a conversation format.	Are partners: ◆ listening to each other? ◆ adding on to each other's ideas? ◆ asking questions of each other? ◆ staying on topic? ◆ engaging in a conversation rather than a share?
Partners look closely at the pictures to support comprehension.	Are partners: ◆ noticing details in the illustrations? ◆ using details in the pictures to add to the story?
Partners observe print conventions.	Are partners using a reading voice that reflects the punctuation, tone, character, rhythm, and other elements of the text?
Partners hold each other accountable for the work.	Are partners: ◆ stopping each other when the text doesn't make sense? ◆ suggesting different word-attack strategies when presented with unfamiliar words? ◆ making and completing reading plans?
Partners think beyond the page to comprehend text.	Are partners: ◆ talking before, during, and after reading texts? ◆ making text-to-self, text-to-text, and text-within-text connections? ◆ debating ideas? ◆ stretching out one another's ideas using words such as "maybe" and "or"?

How to Assess Reading Partnerships

As with all assessment, the assessment of reading partnerships includes a variety of methods. By using a combination of student and teacher assessment techniques, you can gather a great deal of information that highlights the needs and abilities of your partnerships.

Choose the assessment practices that work best for your students. When selecting assessment routines, consider your students' abilities to:
- articulate their thoughts;
- read texts (for early and struggling readers this may include retelling a book from its pictures rather than reading it);
- record written language (e.g., students abilities to record their thinking using sticky notes and graphic organizers); and
- maintain a focus on their work (low stamina and focus may mean that younger students need to meet for shorter sessions).

Below are some assessment practices that help you assess students' talk during daily reading partnerships and reading center partnerships. Because reading partnerships meet on a daily basis, you have continual opportunities to assess the talk students are engaging in with their partners.

◆ READING PARTNERSHIP CONFERENCES ◆

Conferring with partners is an efficient and extremely informative way for you to work with pairs of students. Conferences are unique in that teachers have the opportunity to teach as well as assess what partnerships are doing, as described in Chapter 5. Content, teaching, and coaching conferences are different types of conferences you can use when working with reading partnerships. They are outlined below and explored in depth in Carl Anderson's *How's It Going? A Practical Guide to Conferring With Student Writers* (2000).

Content, teaching, and coaching conferences each serve a different purpose, allowing you to adjust your instruction to meet the needs of each partnership in your class. Each type of conference is illustrated with an excerpt from my own experience or another classroom situation I've observed. A variety of reproducible checklists and open-ended note-taking forms are included on pages 122–125. You'll want to select a recording system for conferring that is easy and useful to you— these notes about partnership reading abilities and areas for future instruction will serve as a resource for planning follow-up mini-lessons and conferences.

> **Managing Assessment Notes**
>
> I keep a three-ring binder for my reading assessment notes. I have a section for each student, which includes multiple copies of the reading assessment reproducible sheet on page 123. Each time I assess a student, I record the date, the type of reading being assessed (e.g., "gr" for guided reading, "pr" for partnership reading, "ic" for individual reading conference), the title of the text, my observations of the student's strengths and weaknesses with talk skills and strategies, and my teaching focus.

Content conference

In a content conference, teachers listen to the substance of partners' talk to evaluate their comprehension and ability to share their ideas in an ongoing partner conversation. Teachers can encourage partners to elaborate on their thinking, to discover what they haven't yet shared or discovered. Using phrases such as "So, can you say more about . . . ?" and "Can you tell me about . . . ?" teachers prompt partners to extend their thinking. Content conferences are best suited for partnerships that have had multiple experiences with specific kinds of books (e.g., same author, style, genre, character). In the excerpt on page 113, notice that the teacher pushes her students to go further with the initial connections they've made and is able to observe a much more expanded conversation.

Teaching conference

In a teaching conference, teachers observe and notice what partners are doing and determine whether students have learned a specific skill. For example, you might say, "So, last time we talked about your trying _____." (Here you name a specific strategy such as making a self-to-text connection with the main character in a book.) Have you been trying to do that? How is it working? Can you show me how you've practiced it in one of the books you've talked about?" If students are still struggling with using the target skill, you can use the conference to reteach the skill or strategy. If they demonstrate proficiency with the skill or strategy, you can take the opportunity to teach a new skill or strategy that has not yet been introduced to the class but is purposeful and appropriate to the work of this partnership. You might say, for instance, to a partnership reading a nonfiction text, "I noticed in your nonfiction book that there were headings at the top of some of your pages and I want to show you how readers use headings to read with a purpose and hold onto the most important information read in the book." An example of a teaching conference is shown on page 114.

◆ Reading Assessment/ Conferring Notes ◆

Date	Teaching Focus	Next Conference	Observations/Setting

123

Partner Reading: A Way to Help All Readers Grow • Scholastic Professional Books

This form helps you record what you've taught and observed and set your agenda for a follow-up conference.

Keep track of each partnership's progress, the focus of your teaching during the conference, and your teaching ideas for the next conference with the reproducible form on page 123. Make multiple copies, assign a sheet to each partnership and keep them on an accessible clipboard that you can carry around the classroom as you confer.

A Partnership Content Conference

Second-grade partners Caiti and Sean have just completed reading Leo the Late Bloomer *by Robert Kraus. The teacher sits beside them and observes their talk.*

Caiti: This book reminds me of the book *The Little Engine That Could,* because Leo is a lot like the Little Engine.

Sean: What do you mean?

Caiti: At first, they both have trouble doing things.

Sean: Yeah, like Leo can't read, write, or draw and the Little Engine can't get up the big hill.

In her anecdotal notes, the teacher records how the partners made connections between two books and encouraged each other to say more about their thinking. The teacher prompts the partners to continue their conversation.

Teacher: Why do you think both the Little Engine and Leo were having trouble doing the things they wanted to do?

Caiti: Maybe because they were young and little.

Sean: Or maybe because it takes a long time to learn to do things like reading and writing. You just don't do them perfectly the first time you try.

Teacher: I wonder why these authors decided to write their stories this way?

Sean: Well, it's interesting when characters in books have a problem and have to try to solve it. Lots of stories we read have characters who have problems.

Caiti: Yeah, and even though these two books are fiction and couldn't really happen, I think the authors are writing them to show us that we shouldn't give up when something is hard.

Teacher: Can you say more about that idea?

Sean: It's like a lot of times when you play something new or try to learn something in school. At first you might have trouble and get frustrated and want to quit.

Caiti: Yeah, like when I tried to ride my two-wheeler. I got mad because everyone made it look so easy, but I just kept falling off. I wanted to put my training wheels back on, but my dad told me to just keep trying. And then a few tries later, I did it!

Sean: Just like Leo and the Little Engine. We should see if the next book we read today also has a character with a problem. . . .

Teacher records in her anecdotal notes the partners' abilities to use text evidence to support their thinking, make self-to-text connections, and make a reading plan. She also notes her teaching focus: using the prompt "Can you say more about that idea?" to push partners to think deeper and longer about an idea.

EXCERPT FROM A PARTNERSHIP TEACHING CONFERENCE

First-grade partners are reading the nonfiction text Ants *(Scholastic).*

Teacher: I notice that when you read simple nonfiction books, you tend to read them quickly and have short conversations. I want to show you a reading strategy called "reading the pictures," which will help you talk about and learn more from nonfiction books, especially those that have only a few words on each page. Let's look at one of the photographs. (*The photograph chosen shows worker ants gathering and bringing food to the queen ant.*) Let's look carefully at the photo. What do you think is happening in the photo? What are the ants doing? (*She guides the partners to focus on the action of the photo.*)

Matthew: They are finding food and carrying it back to the nest.

Teacher: Why do you think they are doing that?

Briana: Maybe because they are worker ants and that's their job.

Teacher: Can we add on to that idea by looking closely at the details in the photo?

Matthew: Well, it looks like there are lots of ants living in the nest, so they need to get a lot of food to feed all the ants.

Teacher: What do you notice about the queen ant?

Briana: She is in charge of the worker ants. They work for her.

Matthew: The queen ant is the boss of the nest. She tells the worker ants to hunt for food and bring it back home. She doesn't hunt for the food.

Briana: It looks like, in a nest, there's only one queen ant and lots of worker ants. I think the queen ant stays in the nest because she is the one who lays the eggs and they don't want her to go out and get hurt . . . .

Teacher: You guys are doing great with the strategy "reading the pictures." You just learned a lot about ants from talking about that one photograph. I want you to try it on the next photo in the book. See if you can discuss three or four things you learn from the photo. Remember that each detail you notice should teach you something about the subject of your book, which is ants.

Teacher records in her anecdotal notes the title and genre of the text the partners are reading and makes notes of her teaching focus—studying photographs to learn more about the subject of a book. During a follow-up reading conference with the partnership, the teacher might ask the partners, "Can you show me how you have been practicing the strategy of 'reading the pictures' with one of your nonfiction books?"

Coaching conference

In a coaching conference, teachers show partners ways they can help one another read and talk about texts. Partners, for example, learn to support one another when reading errors occur. You guide partners to use phrases such as "Does that look right?" "Does that sound right?" and "Does that make sense?" to coach one another to carefully attend to the print and reread the text accurately. (See Chapter 3 for teaching partnerships print strategies.) You can also help partners extend book conversations by teaching them to ask more sophisticated questions such as "Do you think this book is the same as or different from the one we read before? How?" and "How is the character similar to or different from you?"

EXCERPT FROM A PARTNERSHIP COACHING CONFERENCE

First-grade partners have just finished reading Frog and Toad All Year *by Arnold Lobel.*

Teacher: I have noticed that you two have been reading the Frog and Toad series. I was wondering if you could talk long about one of the main characters.

Joe: Well, I noticed that Frog always seems to take care of Toad. In *Frog and Toad All Year*, Frog wakes up lazy Toad and convinces him to go outside and play. In *Days With Frog and Toad*, Frog teaches Toad how to fly his kite when Toad is ready to give up trying.

Teacher: What could you say to your partner to get him to say something about your hunch?

Joe: Can you find other parts in the books where Frog helps Toad?

Mic: Yeah, remember when Frog helped fix Toad's hat and clean his messy house? (*Shows the text illustrations.*)

Joe: That's right. Do you agree that Frog is like the grown-up and Toad is like the kid?

Mic: Well, usually Frog is the adult. But there were a few times that they switched, like in one of the chapters in *Days With Frog and Toad*. Do you remember the part I'm talking about?

Joe: Oh yeah, Toad was worried and went to find Frog and cheer him up. Toad searched everywhere until he found Frog and was sure he was okay, like a parent.

Mic: Right. And also there was a time when Frog was sick in bed and Toad tried to take care of him and keep him company.

Joe: I think we should change our hunch to say usually Frog acts like the parent and takes care of Toad, but sometimes Toad takes care of Frog. What do you think?

The teacher records in her anecdotal notes that the partners are beginning to coach each other to respond and react to each other's ideas, and that they are using text evidence to support their thinking. She notes that she helped partners extend their book conversation by prompting them to ask questions of each other to draw support for their hunch.

HELPFUL CONFERRING TIPS

♦ **Keep records of conferences.** Keep anecdotal notes on conferences. You can use the recorded data to plan upcoming instruction, assess individual student progress, and communicate with parents.

♦ **Build the conference on one instructional focus.** Resist the temptation to teach a multitude of skills during a conference. Rather, select one teaching focus per conference to ensure students take away a specific skill or strategy that will help them read other books.

♦ **Guide partners through a strategy.** Introduce and/or reteach skills and strategies to partnerships as needed and then coach them through the process of using the skill or strategy.

♦ **Make sure conferences are conversations.** Listen as often as you speak. Teachers and partners should have equal conversational roles in conferences.

♦ VIDEOTAPING AND AUDIOTAPING ♦

Using technology, including video cameras and audiocassette players, allows you to capture partner conversations and preserve them, helping you to better manage assessment. Audiotaping partnerships, for example, enables you to assess partner conversations at which you cannot be present. This allows you to assess more than one partnership at a time and helps hold partners accountable for their work. You can listen to and evaluate taped conversations at a later time and provide feedback to partnerships on their talk during a follow-up reading conference.

Also, conversations recorded on video cameras and cassette players can be viewed and heard or transferred to chart paper and shared during mini-lessons to model good talk strategies and practices of partnerships.

♦ READING PARTNERSHIP RECORDING ACTIVITIES ♦

Depending on the age and experience of students, partners can be asked to record their thinking and talking about books in writing. Partners, for example, can use sticky notes to capture the key points of their talk, such as hunches, big ideas, and supporting evidence. By recording short phrases and sentences on sticky notes and placing them accordingly on text pages, partners are better able to hold on to their thinking when sharing their ideas with each other. Reviewing students' ideas in writing also provides you with ongoing examples of the specific work reading partnerships are engaged in, even when you are not present for their book talk. (Chapter 4 identifies a variety of ways sticky notes can be used to mark pages of book talks.)

Graphic organizers are another way students can record ideas discussed as part of their partnership talk. You may want students to use standard graphic organizers such as Venn diagrams, semantic webs, comparison charts, and story maps or create their own organizers to record their thinking and talking.

Partnership projects are another way students can record their thinking and talking about books. Projects work especially well when partners have had multiple experiences with a specific kind of book. Some examples of partnership projects include creating an ABC book after reading a set of ABC books, making a poster-size character web after reading a character series, and making a three-dimensional model of the tadpole life cycle after reading a set of nonfiction texts on tadpoles.

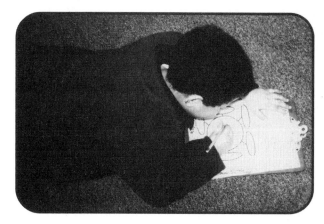

A student records notes on his character web during a character study. He records character traits and details from the texts to support his thinking.

Projects offer an excellent way to motivate as well as assess students on what they have learned through their partnership work. The advantages of assigning projects for assessment are that they allow for different learning styles, encourage decision making and independence as partners decide how best to present their learning, provide appropriate leveling opportunities (projects may vary from simple to complex), encourage creativity, are open-ended, and can be used to teach other partnerships about the texts a partnership has read. (Chapter 6 has a suggested list of ABC study projects partners can do.)

One nonfiction project includes an article on emperor penguins and penguin hand puppets while another project outlines on a poster different bear habitats and "tips for what to do if you encounter a bear." Students have added nonfiction text features such as captions, important vocabulary, and an index.

◆ Benefits of Partnership Recording Activities ◆

Partnership Recording Activity	Assessment Benefits
Comparison Chart/Venn Diagram	Shows partners' ability to compare and contrast two characters, two subjects, and so on.
Semantic Webs	Shows partners' ability to identify character traits, big ideas about characters and subjects, and so on.
Story Mapping	Shows partners' ability to: ◆ retell a story. ◆ sequence story events, the big moments happening to the main character. ◆ identify story elements, including character, setting, plot, change, and movement through time. ◆ differentiate between main ideas and details when summarizing or retelling.
Sticky Notes	Shows partners' ability to use text evidence to support their hunches, big ideas, and connections of texts.
Projects	Shows partners' ability to: ◆ choose and create a project that reflects their abilities. ◆ demonstrate specific knowledge learned about a set of texts. ◆ choose a project style (e.g., poster, graph, book) that will capture their talking and learning.

◆ Reading Partnership Rubrics ◆

Rubrics are an assessment method that both students and teachers can use to evaluate partner work. Rubrics are unique in that students and teachers can brainstorm together the criteria that are included. I have found it helpful to use rubrics early on in the year to emphasize to students what the expectations are of reading partnerships. Recording the criteria in a rubric format helps students clearly distinguish between acceptable and unacceptable partnership practices. When you've established your own criteria for reading partner talk, you'll find it worthwhile to display them on a chart during partnership reading time and then refer to it during mini-lessons, conferences, and shares.

Below is an example of a rubric that reflects behavior expectations set out at the beginning of the year when students are introduced to partnerships.

◆ HOW DID YOUR READING PARTNERSHIP TALK GO TODAY? ◆		
☺ **Good**	☺ **So-So**	☹ **Not Good**
We shared our bag of books.	We had some trouble agreeing on whose books to read.	We argued and didn't take turns sharing our books.
We worked cooperatively to choose ways to read our books.	We only used one kind of reading.	One of us decided how to read every book.
We had a conversation and shared our ideas about the books we read.	Only one of us shared ideas about the books we read.	We talked about things other than our books.

I use role play during my mini-lessons to demonstrate both appropriate and inappropriate behaviors listed on the rubric. I end my mini-lessons giving students explicit instructions on what I've taught by using a phrase such as "So when you and your partner are reading today, make sure to . . . ."

During the share of the daily reading workshop, I ask students to evaluate their partnership work for that session. Students can represent their responses by giving a thumbs-up or down. They can also draw happy, so-so, or sad faces to show whether they met the criteria. Partnerships struggling to meet the criteria can meet on their own or with me to determine ways they can improve their reading practices during follow-up reading sessions.

<table>
<tr><td colspan="4">Name_____ Date_____</td></tr>
<tr><td colspan="4">**Thinking About Being a Good Reading Partner**</td></tr>
<tr><td>Good Partner Strategies</td><td>☺ I always do.</td><td>☺ I sometimes do.</td><td>☹ I never do</td></tr>
<tr><td>Take turns choosing books to read.</td><td></td><td></td><td></td></tr>
<tr><td>Look closely at the pictures.</td><td></td><td></td><td></td></tr>
<tr><td>Look closely at the words.</td><td></td><td></td><td></td></tr>
<tr><td>Help my partner use reading strategies for tricky words.</td><td></td><td></td><td></td></tr>
<tr><td>Add on to my partner's ideas.</td><td></td><td></td><td></td></tr>
<tr><td>Stretch out my ideas.</td><td></td><td></td><td></td></tr>
<tr><td>Share ideas about characters and subjects.</td><td></td><td></td><td></td></tr>
<tr><td>Listen to my partner read and talk.</td><td></td><td></td><td></td></tr>
<tr><td>Disagree in a friendly way.</td><td></td><td></td><td></td></tr>
<tr><td>Make reading plans.</td><td></td><td></td><td></td></tr>
</table>

126

Partner Reading A Way to Help All Readers Grow • Scholastic Professional Books

The reproducible on page 126 lists specific strategies good partners use. Students can check off the column that best describes their proficiency with the strategy. The data you gather can help you observe trouble spots and areas of success more closely and set the focus of the next mini-lesson or partner reading conference.

As the year progresses, I modify our rubrics to reflect new talk strategies and practices students are learning. Below is a rubric I used during our midyear partnership study on ways of extending book conversations.

◆ How Did Your Reading Partnership Talk Go Today? ◆		
☺ **Good**	☺ **So-So**	☹ **Not Good**
We listened to and added on to each other's ideas.	We shared our own ideas without connecting them to our partner's ideas.	We didn't build on each other's ideas or have a conversation.
We asked each other questions to help stretch out ideas.	We changed topics quickly without digging deep and stretching ideas.	We didn't push each other to say more about ideas shared.
We made connections among books, characters, and ideas.	We only made self-to-text connections.	We didn't think beyond the page; we just retold the story.

Partnership Self-Assessment

Periodically throughout the year, I will use our "How Did Your Partnership Talk Go Today?" chart to have students assess their partnerships. These evaluations remind partners of the expectations for productive talk and help them prevent or change poor talk habits.

◆ Reading Partnership Role Playing ◆

Partners who successfully demonstrate a skill, strategy, or habit can role-play as part of a mini-lesson. (You may choose students based on your observations during conferring, videotaping, or audiotaping.) The purpose of students' observation of good partnership role play is to help them transfer these practices to their own reading partnership. By asking the question, "What are these partners doing right?" you can guide the class to notice and name good talk habits and practices. Remember to encourage students to be specific when they describe what they notice a partnership doing well. Students may say, for example, "Each partner looks at the other when speaking," "They ask each other questions when they're confused by what their partner has said," or "Each partner uses what the other one says to say more."

Students may need help from teachers as they learn how to be specific when naming behaviors they are observing. Teachers can model this practice for students by rephrasing what a student says and using specific language such as "The partners are stretching out ideas" and "The partners are adding on to each other's ideas."

◆ REFLECTIONS AND EVALUATIONS ◆

Student evaluation activity sheets can be used for both daily reading and reading center partnerships. Evaluation sheets can be designed to meet your students' needs and are written to help partners reflect on their own partnership behavior as well as that of their partner. You can modify student reflection sheets to target the skills and strategies taught during a unit of study.

Name_____ Date_____

How is Your Reading Partnership Going?

1. My reading partner is _____

2. Our favorite reading spot in the classroom is _____

3. We like to read books about _____

4. I think a good partner is someone who _____

5. My partner helps me by _____

6. How is your partnership going?

☺   😐   ☹

Name: Lily ___ W ___   Date: 3\4\03

Thinking About Our Nonfiction Reading Centers

1. Who was your reading center partner?

   Solange

2. How did you and your partner work together?

   😄   😐   ☹

3. What nonfiction center would you like to be in for our next cycle?

   Cat

4. What was the most interesting thing you learned?

   How the emperera
   penguins be thar age.
   How Penguins slide on ther
   tdmmys when ther in hyres.

During the year, students evaluate their daily reading partnership performance. I modify the form to reflect and assess the new strategies that they've learned. I use the reproducible form on page 127 in October after I've introduced partnership reading.

Each reading center study culminates with students completing a partnership evaluation. I use these assessments to reorganize book baskets and plan the structure of the second cycle.

◆

When you assess reading partners on a consistent basis, you can identify their academic and behavioral strengths and weaknesses and use these data to plan your follow-up instruction. Techniques such as conferring, role-playing, creating rubrics, and audio and video recording can be used to both evaluate and support good partnership practices of your students. Sound assessment practices, in other words, provide you with meaningful data about your students' abilities to understand texts and to engage in purposeful book conversations, which are the essential elements of effective reading partnerships.

◆ Reading Assessment Notes ◆

Student Name:_____

Date	Anecdotal Observations

Partner Reading: A Way to Help All Readers Grow • Scholastic Teaching Resources

◆ Reading Assessment/ Conferring Notes ◆

Date	Teaching Focus	Next Conference	Observations/Setting

Partner Reading: A Way to Help All Readers Grow • Scholastic Teaching Resources

◆ Reading Partnership Skills and Strategies Checklist ◆

Date	Skill Strategy	Observations
	Looks closely at the print.	
	Looks closely at the pictures.	
	Encourages partner to use word attack strategies.	
	Thinks beyond the page.	
	Uses text evidence to support ideas.	
	Records thinking.	
	Adds on to partner's ideas.	
	Stretches out own ideas.	
	Debates in a constructive way.	
	Makes reading plans.	
	Holds partner accountable for work.	

Partner Reading: A Way to Help All Readers Grow • Scholastic Teaching Resources

◆ Reading Partnership Skills and Strategies Checklist ◆

Date	Skill Strategy	Observations

Partner Reading: A Way to Help All Readers Grow • Scholastic Teaching Resources

Name_____ Date_____

Thinking About Being a Good Reading Partner

Good Partner Strategies	☺ I always do.	😐 I sometimes do.	☹ I never do.
Take turns choosing books to read.			
Look closely at the pictures.			
Look closely at the words.			
Help my partner use reading strategies for tricky words.			
Add on to my partner's ideas.			
Stretch out my ideas.			
Share ideas about characters and subjects.			
Listen to my partner read and talk.			
Disagree in a friendly way.			
Make reading plans.			

Name_____ Date_____

How Is Your Reading Partnership Going?

1. My reading partner is _____

2. Our favorite reading spot in the classroom is _____

_____

3. We like to read books about _____

_____

4. I think a good partner is someone who _____

_____

5. My partner helps me by _____

6. How is your partnership going?

Professional References Cited

◆◆◆◆◆◆◆◆◆◆◆◆◆◆

Anderson, C. (2000). *How's it going? A practical guide to conferring with student writers.* Portsmouth, NH: Heinemann.

Cambourne, B. (1988). *The whole story: Natural learning and the acquisition of literacy.* New York: Scholastic.

Collins, K. (2004). *Growing readers: Units of study in the primary class-room.* New York: Stenhouse.

Pinnell, G. & Fountas, I: (1996). *Guided reading: Good first teaching for all children.* Portsmouth, NH: Heinemann.

_____. (1999). *Matching books to readers: Using leveled books in guided reading, K–3.* Portsmouth, NH: Heinemann.

_____. (2001). *Leveled books for readers: Grades 3–6.* Portsmouth, NH: Heinemann.

New Standards: Performance standards. (1997). Washington, DC, and Pittsburgh, PA: National Center on Education and the Economy and the University of Pittsburgh.

Standards for the English language arts. (1996). Newark, DE, and Urbana, IL: National Council of Teachers of English and International Reading Association.

Sulzby, E. & Teale, W. H. (1986). *Emergent literacy: Writing and reading.* Norwood, NJ: Ablex.

Children's Literature Cited

◆◆◆◆◆◆◆◆◆◆◆◆◆◆◆◆◆◆

Agard, J. (1989). *The calypso alphabet.* New York: Henry Holt.

Alda, A. (1993). *Arlene Alda's ABC.* Berkeley: Tricycle.

Andreae, G. (2003). *K is for kissing a cool kangaroo.* New York: Orchard.

Anno, M. (1974). *Anno's alphabet.* New York: Crowell.

Base, G. (1986). *Animalia.* Ringwood, Vic., Australia: Viking Kestrel.

Baskin, L. (1972). *Hosie's alphabet.* New York: Viking.

Bayer, J. (1984). *A, my name is Alice.* New York: Dial.

Bruchac, J. (1997). *Many nations: An alphabet of Native America.* Mahwah, NJ: Bridgewater.

Burningham, J. (1985). *John Burningham's ABC.* New York: Crown.

Calmenson, S. (1993). *It begins with an A.* New York: Hyperion.

Capucilli, A. S. (1996). *Biscuit.* New York: HarperCollins.

Cazet, D. (1998). *Minnie and Moo go to the moon.* New York: DK.

Cowley, J. (1999). *Mrs. Wishy-Washy.* New York: Philomel.

Cushman, D. (1993). *The ABC mystery.* New York: HarperCollins.

Eastman, P. D. (1974). *The alphabet book.* New York: Random House.

Ehlert, L. (1989). *Eating the alphabet.* San Diego: Harcourt Brace Jovanovich.

Eichenberg, F. (1952). *Ape in a cape: An alphabet of odd animals.* New York: Harcourt Brace.

Elting, M. (1980). *Q is for duck.* New York: Houghton Mifflin/Clarion.

Fain, K. (1993). *Handsigns: A sign language alphabet.* San Francisco: Chronicle.

Folsom, M. & Folsom, M. (1985). *Easy as pie.* New York: Clarion.

Fox, M. (1984). *Wilfrid Gordon McDonald Partridge.* Brooklyn, NY: Kane/Miller.

Franco, B. (1994). *Bo and Peter.* New York: Scholastic.

Freeman, D. (1968). *Corduroy.* New York: Viking.

Gág, W. (1993). *The ABC bunny.* New York: Coward, McCann & Geoghegan.

Greven, T. (1995). *Dominie alphabet book.* Carlsbad, CA: Dominie.

Grover, M. (1993). *The accidental zucchini.* San Diego: Browndeer.

Hague, K. (1984). *Alphabears.* New York: Henry Holt.

Hallinan, P. K. (1994). *A rainbow of friends.* Nashville: Ideals.

Henkes, K. (1996). *Lilly's purple plastic purse.* New York: Greenwillow.

Howe, D. & Howe, J. (1979). *Bunnicula.* New York: Atheneum.

Isadora, R. (1983). *City seen from A to Z.* New York: Greenwillow.

J. Paul Getty Museum. (1997). *A is for artist: A Getty Museum alphabet.* Los Angeles: J. Paul Getty Museum.

Jennings, L. (1997). *Penny and Pup.* Wauwatosa, WI: Little Tiger.

Johnson, A. (1989). *A to Z look and see.* New York: Random House.

Johnson, C. (1963). *Harold's ABC.* New York: Harper & Row.

Johnson, S. (1995). *Alphabet city.* New York: Viking.

Kitamura, S. (1992). *From acorn to zoo and everything in between in alphabetical order.* New York: Farrar Straus and Giroux.

Kraus, R. (1971). *Leo the late bloomer.* New York: Windmill/Wanderer.